SURVEY OF LABOR RELATIONS

Second Edition

The first edition of this material was prepared pursuant to Contract #99-8-1383-42-20 from the U. S. Department of Labor by the author, who was commissioned by the George Meany Center for Labor Studies, AFL-CIO, in partial fulfillment of its Tripartite Program for Apprenticeship and Associate Degree in Labor Studies. The opinions contained in this material do not necessarily reflect those of the George Meany Center for Labor Studies, the American Federation of Labor-Congress of Industrial Organizations, or the U. S. Department of Labor.

SURVEY OF LABOR RELATIONS

Second Edition

Lee Balliet

The Bureau of National Affairs, Inc., Washington, D.C.

Second Printing April 1988

Library of Congress Cataloging in Publication Data

Balliet, Lee.
Survey of labor relations.

Bibliography: p.
Includes index.
1. Industrial relations—United States. 2. Trade-unions—United States. 3. Collective bargaining—United States. I. Title.
HD8072.5.B34 1987 331'.0973 87-864
ISBN 0-87179-544-2

Printed in the United States of America
International Standard Book Number: 0-87179-544-2

31

Preface to First Edition

This work could not have been completed without assistance from numerous sources. At the George Meany Center for Labor Studies, Richard Hindle, Irene Kirk, and David Alexander of the Tripartite Program for Apprenticeship and Associate Degree in Labor Studies provided thorough administrative direction to the many tasks involved in producing a textbook of this nature.

Russell Allen, Jacqueline Brophy, Walter Davis, Helmut Golatz, and Reese Hammond, all members of the Tripartite Program's advisory committee, offered many comments and constructive criticisms of early drafts, as did other readers, including John David, Harry Millstone, David Palmer, Jim Payne, Bob Repas, Jim Wallihan, and the numerous students at Bunker Hill Community College, Indiana University, and Rhode Island Junior College, who subjected a final draft of the text to the realities of classroom experience.

Richard Fauss and Michael Parsons assisted with research on various subjects. Special thanks are due to Betty Justice, who contributed much of the research and written material for Chapter 3 on the legal framework of labor relations, and to my wife, Susie Balliet Ross, who put together the material on women workers in Chapter 7 and who also polished the entire copy with her fine editorial skills. I am indebted to all of these people and to any others whose assistance I may have inadvertently failed to acknowledge.

As emphasized in the instructor's guide available to teachers, this text is intended to facilitate learning rather than to serve as a detailed reference work. Therefore, each chapter includes discussion questions and a limited list of suggestions for further reading (full bibliographical information is given in the bibliography), and the instructor's guide lists supplemental teaching aids. Instructors are encouraged to require students to develop individual glossaries of labor relations terms from the "key words and phrases" following each chapter.

Of course, the author alone accepts responsibility for errors and/or omissions which affect the book's usefulness.

LEE BALLIET

Morgantown, W. Va.
March 1980

Preface to Second Edition

Review and revisions for this second edition were completed, primarily, with the able assistance of three individuals. Joe Lawrence, on the staff of AFSCME in Ohio, did much of the preliminary research and drafted additions for most of the chapters. Peter Seybold, Administrative Associate with the Indiana University Division of Labor Studies, lent his fine substantive and editorial skills to the process. And Barbara Lucas typed and proofread the final draft.

Richard Hindle, Joe Harris, and numerous students who used the first edition offered comments and suggestions for the revision. As with the original, however, the author is responsible for any errors or omissions in the second edition.

LEE BALLIET

Bloomington, Indiana
January 1987

Contents

1

Overview and Introduction*

Let him that stole, steal no more, but rather let him labor, working with his hands the thing which is good, that he may have to give to him that needeth.

—Ephesians 4:28

Official government statistics for 1985 set that year's total U.S. production of goods and services at approximately $4 trillion, or nearly $17,000 for each man, woman, and child in the country. By contrast, in 1880, the nation's gross national product (GNP) was $9.2 billion, or $190 per capita; in 1929, it was $103 billion, or $850 per capita. Even allowing for a sevenfold increase in the price level over the past century, it is obvious that our economy has grown enormously in the course of only a century.

Not only has output per capita increased, but, what is more important, so has output per worker. In 1880, the American economy produced about $450 in goods and services per worker; in 1929, just prior to the Great Depression, it was around $2,000 per worker. In 1985, the value of each worker's production averaged almost $35,000 (about $6,000 in 1880 dollars), which represents nearly a thirteenfold increase in productivity (output per worker) over the last 105 years.

Obviously, the nature of our economy has changed a great deal over the years. And so has the nature of work. A hundred and fifty years ago, the typical American worker was a self-employed farmer/entrepreneur, a self-sufficient part of a basically rural economy. Today these circumstances are almost totally reversed. Present-day workers are typically urban dwellers, employees of

*This chapter is based largely on the writings of Butler, Lester, and Sloane and Witney. See Chapter Resources and Bibliography for specific references.

large (most often impersonal) organizations, and highly dependent upon others to provide, for payment, the necessities of life. (See Table 1.)

These historical changes in the nature of work, employment, and life-style are exactly what give rise to our investigation of labor relations. These changes and their consequences are also sources of information for our understanding of the subject. The history of our nation is that of a developing industrial economy. The history of the American people is therefore largely the history of workers, who provided the brain and muscle to build and maintain the nation's productive capacity.

To understand the place of unions and the process of labor-management relations throughout our history, we must remember that America's so-called "captains of industry" (the Carnegies, Goulds, Morgans, Rockefellers, Vanderbilts, etc.) were exactly that; they controlled and directed the efforts and the rewards of their "troops," a labor force composed largely of European immigrants and Americans leaving agriculture to work in a growing industrial economy. In the 50 years between 1877 and 1927, more than 27 million immigrants came to America in search of a new and better life. Also during this period, large numbers of Americans left their farms, usually out of economic necessity, to seek employment in the nation's mines, mills, and factories. These new workers sought economic security and happiness for themselves and their

Table 1. U.S. Population and Labor Force Distribution, 1830, 1880, 1929, 1985

	1830	1880	1929	1985
Population[1]	12,901	50,262	121,767	238,816
Civilian labor force[1]	3,932	17,392	47,757	115,461
Percent of population in labor force	30.5	34.6	39.2	48.3
Distribution (By percent)				
Agriculture	70.5	44.4	22.8	2.9
Nonagriculture	29.5	55.6	77.2	97.1
Unemployed	—[2]	—[2]	3.2	7.2

Source: U.S. Department of Commerce, Bureau of the Census, *Historical Statistics of the United States* (Washington, D.C.: Government Printing Office, 1975); and U.S. Department of Labor, Bureau of Labor Statistics, President's Report for 1986.

[1]In thousands.

[2]Comparable unemployment statistics unavailable.

UAW Solidarity Magazine/Marshall

UAW Solidarity Magazine/Kaufman

UAW Solidarity Magazine/Archives

UAW Solidarity Magazine/Marshall

families. What they most often found was a nightmare of near-starvation wages and frighteningly dangerous working conditions. In general, as in other industrial economies, workers were treated more as beasts of burden than as human beings.

The reactions of workers to such conditions varied, but one principal response was to combine, to join together for protection of their interests and survival. Workers formed labor organizations to promote and defend what they thought were or should be their rights both on and off the job—fair wages, safe working conditions, and, perhaps most important, treatment which reflected respect for them as individuals.

Many of the extreme conditions which originally prompted workers to form and join unions no longer exist, in large part due to union activities. Workers also have benefited from legislative advances, both economic and political, but they join unions today for basically the same reasons they always have. They do not own or control the means of their livelihood and are thus subject to the peculiar whims of their employers. The only direct way they can influence the terms and conditions of their employment is through a collective bargaining agent—a labor organization, a union.

Employers today also resist unions for the same reasons they have historically done so. They view unions as a threat to their authority and control, and, ultimately, their financial success as business owners and managers.

The following chapters will detail the nature and consequences of continuing conflict between workers and employers in the U.S. economy. Before turning to these subjects, however, it will be helpful to discuss some theoretical and practical aspects of the method, organization, and objectives of this study of labor relations.

Establishing an Analytical Framework

The study of labor relations involves all of the social sciences, including political science, sociology, and psychology, but it is primarily concerned with questions of *economic* organization and motivation. The social sciences are based on the same principles of scientific inquiry as the natural sciences, such as physics, chemistry, and biology. The method of scientific inquiry is an attempt to discover logical and observable explanatory relationships. Scientific inquiry, therefore, is based on the processes of definition, formulating theories of interdependence, and testing probable relationships with appropriate tools of analysis.

But the scientific discovery of "truth" depends on attitude as well as method. The scientist and the student must be willing to be open-minded, to consider alternative explanations, and to discard old concepts in light of new findings. These qualities are especially important in the social sciences, where the relationships under investigation are less subject to controlled experimentation. Labor relations, for example, involves an almost unlimited complex of social variables that cannot be isolated or held constant for the purpose of scientific investigation. The possibility of overlooked, omitted, or unavailable data regarding important relationships is greater, which is one reason why different labor observers reach widely differing conclusions about the same events or circumstances.

There are other common pitfalls of which the student and scientist alike must be aware, such as reasoning from the particular to the general, assuming single causation, and allowing value-system biases to influence conclusions.

The dangers of reasoning from the particular to the general are readily apparent. For example, assuming that what is good for some unions is good for all unions, like the advantages of apprenticeship in the building trades, can lead to misunderstanding of important relationships. In practice, this pitfall, which is often referred to as the fallacy of composition, reminds us to be wary of using personal experience as our sole perspective for viewing the larger world.

A similar mistake involves assuming single causation with regard to complex social and economic relationships. For example, it is tempting to attribute union behavior solely to the desire for higher wages and management actions solely to the drive for maximum profits. Such shortsightedness can often result in the illusion of understanding from simple (single-cause) explanations when, in fact, there *is* no single, simple explanation.

An especially critical aspect in sound scientific reasoning is the need to recognize the importance and influence of value-system biases. In the social sciences, it is virtually impossible to disregard totally one's personal experience and feelings. For example, two young people—one a descendant of generations of working coal miners, the other, of generations of coal mine owner/operators—entering college and their first social science classes will probably have quite different perspectives on the nature of work, the place of unions in our society, and the role of government in labor-management relations. In addition to such obvious environmental influences on our thinking, we must also be alert to the tyranny of words. Slogans or phrases such as "union bosses" and "right to work," even such individual words as "strike," "boycott," and "picket" may be laden with emotion, meaning different things to different people. We must always be alert to subjective statements that can mislead us. We must remain as objective as possible.

At the same time, there is nothing wrong or unscientific about reasoning from a particular set of values, so long as they are made explicit. For example, a union organizer would correctly place greater emphasis on the needs of the workers than on an employer's desire to maximize profits. Or, consider the conflict between the welfare of a community and the decision of a company to close a profitable operation which provided the town's main source of employment.

Organization and Objectives: Purpose and Method

Our investigation of labor relations will be something of a stepping-stone or building-block process resulting in a logical conclusion, a better understanding of the present and some guidelines for approaching the future. This chapter concludes with a summary of theories of union development and behavior.

In Chapter 2, the *historical foundations* of the American labor movement are outlined to give us a sense of where we as an industrial society are coming from and thus a better foundation for understanding where we are going. Chapter 3, on the *legal framework* of labor-management relations, provides a more specific historical perspective, primarily because the law and interpretations of the law have been so critical in shaping the form and content of labor relations in our society. Given the legal/historical framework provided by the first three chapters, Chapter 4 details the present *structure* and *function* of American unions. By this point in our investigation, we should have a good background for understanding the *form* of the American labor movement.

Chapters 5 and 6 deal more specifically with the *content* of labor relations, that is, *collective bargaining negotiations* and *contract administration.* These two chapters discuss operational aspects of American unions that make them different from the trade unions of other countries. Finally, Chapter 7 summarizes current problems and trends and speculates on the future of the labor movement in this country and abroad.

It is intended that by the end of this study the reader/student will have a basic understanding of fundamental concepts and procedures of U.S. labor-management relations. Each of the chapter topics is, however, a social science discipline itself, to which many have devoted their entire working lives; therefore we must be careful not to assume that these relatively few pages of text provide all or even the best answers to the topics being discussed.

In addition to the review and discussion questions following each chapter, principal sources and suggestions for further reading are listed for the reader who wishes to pursue a particular topic.

Theories of Union Development and Behavior

Before looking in detail at various aspects of the American labor movement, a review of several alternative explanations of union development and behavior is in order. Obviously the term "labor movement" implies something more than the existence of numerous unions. The concept of a labor movement suggests an entity in itself, with goals and objectives, with an organizational personality that is more than simply the sum of its many parts. Numerous scholars have attempted to explain this concept via their theories of labor union development—covering such questions as why unions are formed and why workers join (or do not join) unions—and patterns of union development and behavior in establishing and accomplishing various goals in different industries and geographic areas.

An early theory of the American labor movement was developed in the 1920s by Robert Hoxie of the University of Chicago. Hoxie divided unions into *structural* and *functional* types, depending on industrial and worker-group perspectives. He identified four principal types of unionism:

(1) *Business unionism* stresses trade-conscious rather than class-conscious goals and tactics. Business unionism is identified with immediate job-related issues, such as wages, hours, and working conditions, and gives little attention to political and social welfare activities unless related to basic economic objectives.

(2) *Revolutionary unionism,* almost the exact opposite of business unionism, is based on class-conscious rather than trade-conscious objectives. Revolutionary unions are usually part of a larger political movement designed to do away with capitalist institutions, such as private ownership of resources and capitalist control of the means of production, replacing them with worker-controlled industrial organizations.

(3) *Friendly* or *uplift unionism* has as its goal the enhancement of the moral and social welfare of workers. It concentrates on mutual benefit activities, such as political activity and cooperative enterprises, to accomplish its objective.

(4) *Predatory unionism's* main characteristic is the ruthless pursuit of immediate gains, usually economic, and usually for the persons who run these unions rather than for the workers themselves, without regard to ethical or legal considerations. Obviously this type of union most closely resembles what are today considered "corrupt" unions.

In the late 1920s at the University of Wisconsin, Selig Perlman developed his theory of the labor movement after analyzing union development in England, Germany, Russia, and the United States. His model of union behavior is based on three facets of modern industrial development. First is the historical resistance of business owners (capitalists) to organized workers' movements. Second is the degree of influence over the labor movement by intellectuals who urge workers to lay aside their job-conscious goals and opt for radical (socialistic) changes at the workplace. Third is the maturity of the trade union perspective in regard to the realities of capitalist and intellectual motivation and behavior. Perlman's theory suggests that the nature of the labor movement in a given society at a given time will depend on the relative strength of these three determining factors—capitalist resistance, intellectual influence, and union maturity—and that as historical and political circumstances change, so will the labor movement.

An excellent example of intellectual influence on the development of a nation's labor movement can be seen in the labor movement theory of British labor economists Beatrice and Sidney Webb, who were active in the formation of England's Labour Party in the early 1900s. The Webbs theorized that workers originally join unions for purely economic reasons but that ultimately the labor movement must turn to basic political and economic reforms, such as the nationalization of major industries, to accomplish its goals. They developed their theory and worked for its application within an ideological framework of socialism. The Webbs were instrumental in drafting the original socialistic platform of the Labour Party but did not live to see the attainment of many of its goals after World War II, when the party controlled the national government.

Another European's theory of the labor movement, one which has greatly influenced the course of world history, is that of the German social philosopher Karl Marx. Unlike the Webbs, with their idea of a peaceful political transition to socialism, he envisioned revolutionary worker seizure of the means of production. According to Marx the very nature of capitalism, with its drive for profit and capital accumulation, brings unions into existence as workers combine to resist employer efforts to keep wages as low as possible. His ultimate goal was the establishment of a form of economic organization where social needs prevailed over the logic of profit as a basis for decision making. Although controversy continues over the applicability of Marxist theory to modern-day industrial capitalism, it is thought provoking, especially for those of us in capitalistic societies, that in 1986 more than a third of the world's population lives and works in predominantly socialistic economies.

A recent theory relating the labor movement to the worldwide process of industrialization was formulated by four notable American economists—Clark Kerr, John T. Dunlop, Frederick H. Harbison, and Charles A. Myers—and published in their classic *Industrialism and Industrial Man.* The labor movement theory of the "four horsemen," as they have come to be known, is premised on the inevitability of industrialization as the universal means of solving the problem of meeting human needs and wants. However, they theorize that industrialization and the commitment/reaction of workers to it have taken different forms, depending on the nature of the society (and its controlling leadership, or elite) in which economic development takes place.

Kerr, Dunlop, Harbison, and Myers identify from history five eco-governmental elites (dynastic, colonial, middle-class, revolutionary intellectual, and nationalist) which, because of differing economic, social, and political conditions, necessarily approach economic development and industrialization in different ways, prompting various but predictable controls over workers and worker responses to those controls. They suggest that the world is moving toward what they call "pluralistic industrialism," a higher form of economic and political contest between the forces of technological uniformity and those of individual diversity. They assert that the benefits of technology can and will increasingly be made to serve the needs of people everywhere, that industrialism will finally homogenize present-day economic and political differences among nations. They conclude that despite inevitable and continuing conflict between managers and the managed, global peace will ultimately prevail from the realization of the universal benefits of industrial progress.

Their theory, however, was advanced in 1960, at a time when

the American economy and middle class were both expanding; when the "green revolution" was taking hold in the Third World; and when war, though far from eliminated, had somewhat abated.

But in the next quarter century, there emerged once again the other Four Horsemen, those of the Apocolypse: War, Famine, Pestilence, and Death—albeit in a more modern guise. Starvation today ravages much of Africa; Southeast Asia has been reduced to a killing field; and technology's premier achievement seems to have been reducing the relatively few minutes left on the Doomsday Clock. The march of industrialization brought with it Bhopal, Love Canal, and Chernobyl.

The inevitable conflict between manager and managed has frequently been heightened rather than eased by industrial and technological advances. Technology has just as often deskilled workers and debased their power as it has enhanced their knowledge, sense of worth, and control over their lives. Industrialism's reward frequently has been a dubious consumerism, the price of which can be viewed as a hidden charge on human progress.

The time-honored vehicle for collective action and benefit, the labor movement, has in this country been staggered by a combination of external forces and its own frailities. Beginning in the late 1970s, the level of employer hostility toward unions increased dramatically and continued unabated into the mid 1980s. These attacks have created serious problems for the overall strength and progress of the American labor movement. In response, workers and unions have been forced to reassess many of their long-standing beliefs about the fairness of the U.S. system of labor relations.

With these different perspectives on the formation and prospects of unions in mind, we turn now to the historical foundation of the labor movement in the United States.

Key Words and Phrases

business unionism	nationalization of industry
capital accumulation	natural science
capitalism	output per capita
consumerism	pluralistic industrialism
fallacy of composition	predatory unionism
gross national product	productivity
industrialism	revolutionary unionism
industrialization	scientific inquiry
industrializing elites	single causation
labor force	social science
labor movement	socialism
maturity of the trade union perspective	uplift unionism
means of production	value-system biases

Review and Discussion Questions

1. In general, is the U.S. economy today more productive than 100 years ago? If so, why might that be?

2. From the material in this chapter, it is obvious that the nature of the U.S. labor force has changed considerably over the past 100 years. What were the major changes mentioned? Do you think the nature of the labor force and of work is still changing in our economy? If so, why and in what ways?

3. Do you agree, as stated in this chapter, that workers today join unions for much the same reasons that they joined unions 100 years ago? Why or why not?

4. What are the basic differences between capitalism and socialism? Are these differences fundamentally economic or political in nature?

5. Review the principal processes of scientific inquiry and the pitfalls to sound reasoning mentioned in this chapter.

6. In your opinion, which of the labor movement theories mentioned in this chapter may be most applicable to the U.S. labor movement? Why?

Chapter Resources and Suggested Further Reading

Complete bibliographical information for the following titles can be found in the Bibliography.

Bloom and Northrup, "The Nature of Labor Problems," in *Economics of Labor Problems.*

Butler, "Labor in the Economy," and "Theory of Unions," in *Labor Economics and Institutions.*

Cohen, "Sources of Labor Supply," and "The Labor Force Today," in *Labor in the United States.*

Freeman and Medoff, *What Do Unions Do.*

Kerr, Dunlop, Harbison, and Myers, *Industrialization and Industrial Man.*

Lekackman and Van Loon, *Capitalism for Beginners.*

Lester, "Keys to Labor Knowledge," in *Economics of Labor.*

Marshall, Briggs, and King, *Labor Economics, 5th Edition.*

Rius, *Marx for Beginners.*

Sloane and Witney, "Organized Labor and the Management Community: An Overview," in *Labor Relations.*

Labor is prior to, and independent of, capital. Capital is the fruit of labor, and could never have existed if labor had not first existed.

—Abraham Lincoln, 1859

Without labor nothing prospers.

—Sophocles, circa Fifth Century

A society that gives to one class all the opportunites for leisure, and to another all the burdens of work, dooms both classes to spiritual sterility.

—Lewis Mumford, 1940

Labor, even the most humble and the most obscure, if it is well done, tends to beautify and embellish the world.

—Gabrielle D'Annunzio, 1920

2

Historical Foundations of the American Labor Movement*

When the Union's inspiration through the workers' blood shall run
There can be no power greater anywhere beneath the sun.
Yet what force on earth is weaker than the feeble strength of one?
But the Union makes us strong.

—Ralph Chaplin, 1912

According to the annals of history, American unions were due to celebrate their bicentennial before that of the nation in 1976. There are recorded accounts of the existence of trade unions prior to the American Revolution. The printers are known to have struck the New York *Royal Gazette* in 1778. In 1779, there was a seamen's strike in Philadelphia, and during the 1780s, efforts by workers to organize and confront their employers over the terms and conditions of employment became more and more numerous. Admittedly, most of these early efforts were short-lived, but they mark the beginning of what is by now more than 200 years of American labor history. Unions in the 1980s are certainly the cumulative result of this long history; their nature and functions today reflect two centuries of experience (both success and failure) with U.S. economic and industrial development.

The predecessors of present-day unions as we know them were craft guilds. Beginning in Europe during the Middle Ages, guilds were formed by persons in a single craft to establish professional

*This chapter is based largely on the writings of Boyer and Morais, Brooks, and various public documents. See Chapter Resources and Bibliography for specific references.

standards and to provide mutual aid and assistance to members in need. They were not unions as we think of them, since they included both workers (apprentices and journeymen) and employers (masters). Collective bargaining was an unknown concept in the guilds.

The First Trade Unions

It is important to note that when organizations comprised solely of employees finally made their appearance in the mid-to late-eighteenth century, like the guilds they were formed by skilled craft workers (carpenters, shoemakers, printers, etc.) far more often than by relatively powerless factory workers, of whom there were very few at the time. In a growing economy still comprised of small local production units, the extension of transportation and markets beyond an isolated local community brought a new era of product and labor competition to the American economy. Skilled craft workers recognized the threat of "imported" goods and an expanding labor market, with their accompanying competitive pressures on wages and apprenticeship and quality (professional) standards. They also recognized that they were often in an advantageous position to make demands upon their employers (masters), primarily because of the relative scarcity of skilled labor in eastern markets resulting from the expansion of the western frontier and the consequent draining of the local (eastern) labor supply.

The first unions of craft workers made relatively few but remarkably modern-sounding demands on employers. Principally, they sought to protect and/or advance wages (or their "price scale," as it was known at the time), control the use of apprentices in the production process, and, as a way of further protecting these basic interests, require their employers to hire union members exclusively (the closed shop). Like the guilds, many of these early unions also established benefit society (funeral, sickness) functions for their members.

But early unions did not bargain with their employers in the modern sense of the word. They presented employers with lists of demands that, when economic conditions were favorable, might be met, perhaps after a strike or other "job action." When conditions were less favorable, the unions made fewer demands, knowing that employers were likely to win any protracted struggle by replacing strikers, who would then have difficulty finding new employment.

Permanent unions (worker organizations lasting beyond an immediate and particular set of demands) began to appear in the decade of the 1790s, a 10-year period when workers were increasingly confronted by employer demands for wage cuts at the same time that the cost of living was increasing some 30 percent. Such unions were established between 1792 and 1818 in the larger cities (New York, Boston, Philadelphia, Baltimore, Washington, D.C., New Orleans, etc.) by cordwainers (shoemakers), printers, tailors, carpenters and cabinetmakers, masons, and coopers. Their goals and tactics became longer range. In addition to control of apprenticeship, they worked to establish minimum wages in their locale. In addition to direct economic strikes, secondary boycotts were used for the first time to publicize demands and seek community support, especially from other workers.

Employers, however, did not sit by idly while unions formed around and within their industries. They began to organize their own associations to develop strategy and tactics for resisting the demands of workers. Their most successful weapon for breaking worker uprisings, and one which has persisted to the detriment of modern-day unions, was the legal (court) interpretation and enforcement of their property rights and privileges as employers over the rights of their employees to form and join unions to advance their own interests.

In 1806, the Journeyman Cordwainers Society of Philadelphia was declared by local police courts to be, *by its very existence*, a combination in restraint of trade—its membership constituting a *criminal conspiracy* intended to inflict economic injury upon the employer(s), who had filed suit during a strike for higher wages and improved working conditions. The "cordwainer doctrine," as it came to be known in numerous other similar cases in the next few years, virtually precluded the possibility of a legally protected labor organization. This doctrine strongly influenced the course of union growth for the next 36 years, until 1842.

A second major impediment to early union growth and development was the periodic occurrence of economic depressions such as that of 1819, the first faced by the fledgling union movement. In times of economic adversity, employers were quick to exercise their power when jobs were at a premium. They cut wages and were especially harsh toward workers who had joined unions at earlier, more prosperous times. By 1821, what unions remained were virtually at the mercy of employers and their supporters in the courts.

The return of economic prosperity in late 1822 brought with it renewed union organizing on an even broader scale than before the depression. Skilled craft workers organized and reorganized in spite of the constant threat of the cordwainer doctrine, both in the established eastern cities and in the newer cities of the West (Buffalo, Pittsburgh, Cincinnati, and Louisville). And the beginnings of factory unions appeared. For the first time as well, significant numbers of women workers became active in the movement. In 1825, the United Tailoresses of New York, a trade union for women only, was formed in New York City.

Amid new conspiracy trials in Philadelphia (the tailors in 1827 and the spinners in 1829), a labor movement was born in that city in 1827, when 15 different trades formed the nation's, and probably the world's, first central labor union (the Philadelphia Mechanics Union of Trade Associations) to coordinate their activities on a citywide basis. One of the Philadelphia association's first objectives was the attainment of a 10-hour workday for its members. The following year, it converted itself into a political party and began endorsing labor candidates for public office.

The Era of Labor Parties and City Central Bodies

Unfavorable court decisions and another setback from economic depression in the late 1820s and early 1830s prompted the era of labor parties (1827–1837), in which workers attempted to find political solutions to their economic problems. In addition to the Mechanics Union in Philadelphia, labor parties were formed in New York, Boston, Newark, Pittsburgh, and other large cities. The various party platforms included many demands directed at what workers perceived as reasons for their relative powerlessness in a growing industrial (wage-labor) economy. They sought universal male suffrage, equal and universal education, a mechanic's lien law,[1] and abolition of the militia system, imprisonment for debt, and chartered monopolies (especially banks). But the labor parties failed for a variety of reasons, including factionalism and attacks by the major political parties. Perhaps most significant was the preemption of workers' demands by the political followers of Andrew Jackson, who took much of their own platform from the labor parties.

The temporary renewal of economic prosperity in 1832 hastened the return of workers to trade associations and city central

[1]A mechanic's lien is a legal right to hold property or have it sold to pay for services performed.

bodies. The Philadelphia Mechanics Union had disbanded during the depression of 1828–1831 but was revived in the three years following 1832, along with other and new central bodies in at least 15 cities. These organizations represented a new peak in union activity, if only for a brief period. They began to publish their own newspapers and conducted a series of generally successful strikes for higher wages and shorter working hours (the 10-hour day). Once again, however, and this time in what was the nation's most severe and long-lasting depression to date (1837–1850), the labor movement fell apart in the midst of economic adversity.

The Emergence of National Unions

Just prior to the panic of 1837, efforts to form *national* unions had begun in a number of crafts. In 1834, a national crafts association, the National Trades Union (NTU), had been formed in New York City and included most of the existing city central bodies. The NTU urged the creation of more trade associations and the establishment of a 10-hour day for craft workers employed by the Federal Government.

The first national single-craft union, the National Typographical Society, was organized in 1835. Others followed shortly thereafter among shoemakers, comb makers, carpenters, and handloom weavers. But neither the NTU nor any of the other single-craft national unions weathered the long economic storm of the 1840s. Again workers were forced to wait for the return of economic prosperity before they could advance their goals of union organization.

Not all had been lost during the long years of depression, however. In 1840, by executive order, President Martin Van Buren established a 10-hour day for federal employees on public works; in 1842, Massachusetts and Connecticut passed laws prohibiting children from working more than 10 hours per day; in 1847, New Hampshire was the first state to legally establish the 10-hour workday; and in 1848, Pennsylvania set the minimum age for workers in some commercial establishments at 12 years, raising it to 13 years in 1849.

Most important to the labor movement as a whole was the Massachusetts Supreme Court case of *Commonwealth v. Hunt* (1842), which effectively overturned the cordwainer doctrine. The court ruled that unions were not, per se, illegal organizations and that to be found guilty of conspiracy a union would have to be engaged in criminal activity or be of criminal purpose. The court also ruled that efforts to establish a closed shop were neither unlawful nor proof of unlawful purpose.

Commonwealth v. Hunt gave great impetus to union organizing once economic conditions improved in the early 1850s. Instead of assuming that the mere formation of a union was illegal, unions became subject to the "means" test; that is, each case of supposed illegal activity had to be treated on its own merit, and the union proved guilty of some specific criminal purpose or act. In this new era of relative enlightenment, at least until the depression of 1857, there was a flurry of new national union formation. In 1852, the Typographical Union, the first such national organization to endure to the present, was established. The Hat Finishers Union was organized in 1854, the Journeyman Stonecutters Association in 1855, the United Cigar Makers in 1856, and the Iron Molders (forerunner of the present-day Molders and Allied Workers Union) and Machinists and Blacksmiths in 1859.

But almost predictably, depression took its toll of unions, beginning in 1857, along with increasing signs of civil war, which finally erupted in 1861. However, the false prosperity of a wartime economy prevented the destruction of unions on as large a scale as had previously been the case, and the Molders Union survived, encouraging organization of others, especially in the booming railroad industry (Locomotive Engineers, 1863; Conductors, 1868; and Firemen and Enginemen, 1873). In 1866, a new federation of trade unions, the National Labor Union (NLU), was organized. Under the dedicated leadership of its first president, William Sylvis of the Molders Union, the NLU agitated for the eight-hour workday and the protection and equal pay of women workers. It led organizing drives throughout the nation, but like its predecessor the NTU, it was unable to survive a depression, this time in 1873.

Confrontation and Competition in a New Industrial Order

The post-Civil War era marked a turning point in American economic history, and, as a consequence, in the history of labor-management relations. Prior to the 1860's, growth in the nation's economy had been steady, even though punctuated by a series of recessions and depressions. The completion of the transcontinental railroad in 1869 was but one major achievement in the process of establishing a truly national and increasingly industrial economy, prompted in large part by the Civil War's need for large-scale production and its eventual opening of new resource and product markets. The nation's population nearly quadrupled in the 50 years from 1830 to 1880. During the same period, its nonagricultural labor force increased more than eightfold, from 1.16 million to 9.97 million (see Table 1, p. 2).

As the pace of industrialization picked up, so did the problems of both industrial and craft workers. In response to protections given unions as a result of *Commonwealth v. Hunt,* employers stepped up their efforts to discourage union organizing through such tactics as firing union sympathizers and forming secret employer societies to carry out antiunion strategy. Rapid industrial expansion was marked by the growth of giant corporate and financial trusts whose collective attitude was contemptuous of workers as well as of the public welfare in general. One response on the part of workers was to form their own secret societies, such as the Molly Maguires in the anthracite coalfields and the Knights of St. Crispin among shoemakers.

The 1870s and 1880s were not only decades of great upheaval involving both success and failure for the labor movement; they were also years in which the character of the labor movement for many decades to come was formulated. In addition to the openly growing hostility of employers on virtually all fronts, workers and their unions faced an organizational dilemma. The need for a nationally organized labor movement was obvious. The issue was whether such an organization should be based on the direct affiliation of local unions and city central bodies cutting across trade lines or on a confederation of national trade or craft unions, each maintaining its own autonomy and jurisdiction. The direct affiliation approach, which had been tried unsuccessfully several times, was championed by the Knights of Labor, the autonomous union approach by the American Federation of Labor after its founding in the 1880s.

In 1836, just prior to the beginning of a 13-year economic depression, union membership totaled some 300,000 (6.5 percent of the labor force). In 1872, after two major and one minor depression and a five-year Civil War (which had actually encouraged union growth), union membership was still 300,000, but only 2.1 percent of a much larger labor force. The panic of 1873, prompted by the "bankruptcy" of Jay Cooke and Company (underwriters of the Northern Pacific Railroad), began another five years of depression that severely tested the strength and determination of union organization.

Employers were quick to seize upon the situation to rid themselves of the union "menace." They slashed wages, fired and blacklisted union sympathizers, and increasingly recruited immigrant workers who were more easily discouraged from union organization. Significantly, employers also increased their efforts to develop technology that would allow them to substitute unskilled for skilled workers and women and children for men.

The post-Civil War era of economic development began a siege of labor-management violence unknown before in history. The violence of employers was demonstrated by their almost total lack of concern for human rights and dignity, especially with regard to child labor:

> These little fellows [breaker boys][1] go to work in this cold dreary room at 7:00 in the morning and work till it is too dark to see any longer. For this they get $1 to $3 a week. One result of their work is clean, fresh coal, that burns away to ashes in the grate; another result I found in a miners' graveyard, beside a pretty little church, where more than every other stone bears the name of some little fellow under fifteen years of age.[2]

Workers such as the Molly Maguires in the anthracite coalfields responded with a violence of their own in protest against such degrading conditions. The Molly Maguires terrorized the coalfields, only, in the end, to be broken up by labor spies and usually false murder charges. At least 19 anthracite coalfield union leaders were hanged in the mid-1870s, often after being found guilty in courts controlled or headed by coal operators. But no coal operator was ever convicted of violence against workers who were maimed or killed in the mines.

In 1877, four years into the depression, a proposed wage cut by the Baltimore and Ohio Railroad prompted widespread strikes and riots by rail workers. The uprisings were finally crushed with the help of federal militia and a new employer weapon, the court injunction, but not until scores of workers and citizens had been killed and wounded. In Baltimore and Pittsburgh alone, the death toll stood at 33.

When economic recovery began anew in 1878, the ranks of union labor had dwindled to some 50,000, one sixth of its strength only five years earlier. But in spite of reduced numbers, there were growing signs of labor unrest and rebellion against worsening con-

[1]Breaker boys removed slate and other impurities from coal during the grading process.

[2]Quoted in Anthony Bimba, *The Molly Maguires* (New York: International Publishers, 1932), p. 31.

ditions in the mines, the mills, and the factories. The Greenback-Labor Party, a merger of the Greenback Party and the Workingmen's Party, was formed in 1878 and began advocating political solutions for the problems of farmers and wage earners. But much of its program was adopted by another organization more closely resembling a labor union which had been founded in Philadelphia in 1869 by Uriah Stephens, a tailor, as a secret society for both skilled and unskilled workers.

The Knights of Labor: One Big Union

The Noble and Holy Order of the Knights of Labor admitted to membership any and all, regardless of race or creed, who worked with their hands as "producers," except liquor dealers, bankers, stockbrokers, professional gamblers, lawyers, and other so-called "economic parasites." Its goal was the establishment of one big union in which farmers, shopkeepers, and small employers would join with wage earners, both craft and industrial, to expose the evils of capitalism and to replace capitalist exploitation with worker/producer cooperatives.

After a new constitution eliminated its secrecy provisions in 1878–1879, the Knights began a seven-year period of spectacular growth—increasing their membership from 52,000 in 1883 to 700,000 in 1886—the like of which had never before been seen in this or any other industrial nation. Under the leadership of Terence V. Powderly, a spellbinding orator, the Noble and Holy Order championed both economic and political solutions in behalf of all those "of honorable toil." Its objectives, in addition to the establishment of cooperatives, included the eight-hour day, homesteading on public lands, monetary expansion, prohibition of child labor, adult education, and income and inheritance taxes.

Powderly was opposed to direct strike action by workers, preferring compulsory arbitration (what today would be considered mandatory bargaining with a no-strike clause). But the tide of events beginning in 1884 with depression and wage cutting swept Powderly's desire aside. In 1885, workers, many of them Knights, conducted two highly successful strikes against wage cuts on the midwest railroad system controlled by Jay Gould. The second strike represented the first time an American industrial giant was forced to recognize a union. During the same year, some 200 worker boycotts erupted, nearly all of them supported by the Knights. Membership expanded by more than half a million in little more than a

Breaker boys at the mine remove slate from the coal.
Carnegie Library, Pittsburgh, Pa.

Holding strikers in check during the textile strike in Lawrence, Mass. 1912.
Library of Congress

year, and at one point Powderly called a 40-day moratorium on accepting new assemblies (locals). Success brought chaos to the highly centralized organization of the Noble and Holy Order.

As early as 1880, signs of dissent and division appeared within the all-inclusive membership of the Knights that would soon cause it to collapse almost as quickly as it had risen to prominence. The goal of the Knights of Labor was to find a workable substitute for corporate capitalism, namely, for all workers to become self-employed "worker capitalists." But the interests of farmers and shopkeepers differed from those of unskilled and semiskilled industrial workers. And the interests of skilled craft workers represented a third distinct group, far removed from the other two. The Knights tended to disregard craft lines, while the craft unions appealed directly to the self-interest of skilled workers. The Knights regarded strikes as disruptive to the attainment of their long-range goals, but the craft unions saw direct worker action as a powerful tool for increasing their bargaining strength. By comparison, the Knights of Labor represented a challenge to corporate capitalism while the craft unions either bypassed or accepted corporate capitalism as a fact of American industrial life, to be dealt with pragmatically.

In 1881, the craft unions had organized the Federation of Organized Trades and Labor Unions. The Federation was primarily a political organization patterned after the British Trades Union Congress. It sought to advance the interests of skilled craft workers but floundered for five years amid the heyday of the rapidly growing Knights of Labor. At its 1884 convention, the Federation resolved that the eight-hour day should begin on May 1, 1886. Considering the lack of strength of the organization, this was a meaningless gesture, but regardless of purpose or intent, the declaration became a key factor in the decline of the Knights of Labor and the rise of the American Federation of Labor, which developed from the Federation of Organized Trades and Labor Unions in 1886.

Early in 1886, Gould employees on the Missouri Pacific and Missouri, Kansas, and Texas Railroads struck for the eight-hour day and $1.50 per day "for all laboring men." This time, however, after his defeats in the Midwest a year earlier, Gould—with the help of other Wall Street rail interests—was ready and anxious for a showdown with the Knights. In the end, the Knights' executive board was forced to accept defeat and call off the strike on May 4, the same day that tragic events in Chicago brought an end to the growing eight-hour movement among workers in that city and elsewhere.

On May Day, 1886, 40,000 workers (many of them members of Knights of Labor assemblies) struck for the eight-hour day in Chicago, part of an estimated 300,000 nationwide. Tens of thousands had already been granted the shorter workday without a strike. The situation nationwide was tense as employers recruited strikebreakers and solicited police protection for them. In Chicago on May 3, police had opened fire on strikers harassing "scabs" at the McCormick Reaper works, killing at least four and wounding many others. At a mass meeting on the evening of May 4 in Chicago's Haymarket Square to protest the McCormick shootings, a still unknown person threw a bomb into the midst of 180 policemen trying to break up the peaceful meeting; 66 were wounded, seven of whom later died. The police fired into the crowd repeatedly, killing several and wounding some 200. Although there was no evidence connecting any of them with the Haymarket bombing, eight of Chicago's labor leaders were arrested and charged with the murder of one of the policemen who had died. Four were hanged (August Spies, Adolph Fischer, George Engel, and Albert Parsons), one (Louis Lingg) committed suicide the day before his scheduled execution, and the remaining three (Michael Schwab, Samuel Fielden, and Oscar Neebe) were pardoned seven years later by newly elected Illinois Governor John Altgeld, who called the whole incident "an irreparable and monstrous legal wrong."

But the damage had been done. The terror and executions of the Haymarket tragedy crushed the eight-hour movement, its leadership, unions in general, and the Knights of Labor in particular. Terence Powderly refused to join any public appeal for clemency, fearing that the Knights would be associated with violence and anarchy. In the next two years, most employers reimposed the 10- and 12-hour workday. The newly formed American Federation of Labor later set May 1, 1890, as the date for another mass effort to attain the eight-hour day.

The AFL—Business Unionism Prevails

Gould's victory in the Southwest and the chilling effects of Haymarket were severe blows to the Knights of Labor. But the growing dissatisfaction of craft-union leadership with the Knights' all-inclusive and centralized organization caused the collapse of the Noble and Holy Order as a significant force in the labor movement.

The craft unions, led by Peter McGuire of the United Brotherhood of Carpenters and Joiners (formed in 1881) and Adolph Strasser and Samuel Gompers of the Cigar Makers (formed in 1864), had become locked in a life-or-death struggle with the Knights. At the 1886 Knights convention, anti-craft-union factions solidified their control of the organization, thus prompting the call for formation of the AFL in December of that year in Columbus, Ohio.

At the founding convention of the American Federation of Labor, the craft unions finally had their way. They were the only ones there. The principles of formation reflected their long-standing disagreement with the Knights' philosophy. First and foremost, one, but only one, national union would be chartered in each craft or trade jurisdiction, and this union would be autonomous within the Federation, free to establish its own admission, apprenticeship, and bargaining policies. Second, the AFL pledged to avoid any and all permanent political alliances and long-range reformist (political) programs, instead concentrating on immediate wage gains and other job-related issues, engaging in politics only, in Gompers' words, to "reward labor's friends and defeat labor's enemies." Third, the strike was sanctioned as a legitimate and effective pressure tactic for attaining job-related gains for skilled craft workers.

Thus, while the Knights were inclusive, the AFL was exclusive. The Knights sought to combine *all* workers and to do away with capitalist exploitation; the AFL's efforts were directed at improvements for *skilled* workers within the capitalist system. In the end, which came very shortly for the Knights, the exclusive business unionism of the AFL won out over inclusive schemes to eliminate the wage system. By 1890, membership in the Knights of Labor had fallen to 100,000, and by the turn of the century the organization was almost extinct—to the delight of Gompers and the AFL as well as of industrial employers throughout the land.

Employers in the growing manufacturing sector had been shocked by the mass movement of the eight-hour strikes in the mid-1880s. And they vowed to crush the growing industrial union movement. In large part, the fledgling AFL survived the turbulent years on either side of the turn of the century because employers realized that skilled workers were less easily replaced than the unskilled, and that skilled workers were a relatively small and dwindling proportion of the total labor force. Employer organizations were formed to fight industrial unions, making liberal use of lockouts, strikebreakers, armed guards, company spies, and, ultimately, the U.S. Government.

Membership gains in the AFL were significant, even in comparison to those of the Knights just a few years earlier. AFL membership rose from 140,000 at its founding to 278,000 in 1898, to 1.6 million in 1904, although the latter increase came in large part from affiliation of already established unions. The real potential for growth, however, was among industrial and non-craft workers. With the decline of the Knights, these workers found themselves increasingly frustrated by worsening job conditions and with no established organization to organize or assist them.

Depression once again wracked the country for five long years from 1893 to 1898, and once again employers responded with broad-scale wage cutting. There were valiant attempts by industrial workers to organize and combat their condition, but at the same time, the opponents of an industrial union movement redoubled their efforts to assure its failure. For example, in 1892, at the Homestead, Pa., works of Carnegie Steel (later to become U.S. Steel), 300 hired Pinkerton guards fought workers protesting a 25-percent wage cut, killing seven and wounding scores. Twenty-seven strike leaders were indicted for treason against the state of Pennsylvania. Although they were later vindicated in court, the union treasury had been depleted, and the steel industry continued to reduce wages and lengthen working hours. Fifteen years later, nonunion steel mill laborers were paid $1.65 for a 10-hour day and $1.98 for a 12-hour day, compared to $2.36 for an eight-hour day earned by unionized common laborers in nearby bituminous coal mines.

Industrial Union and Radical Left Challenges to the AFL

In 1894, workers at the Pullman Company near Chicago finally struck out of desperation over 25-percent wage cuts (with no reduction in rents for Mr. Pullman's company-owned housing) and joined the American Railway Union (ARU), which had been founded the year before by Eugene Victor Debs. In its first year, the ARU, an industrial union of railroad employees, had grown to 150,000 members—half those of the entire AFL. At its first convention, for two weeks beginning June 12, 1894, Debs succeeded in quelling a delegate call for sympathy strikes in support of the Pullman workers and appointed an ARU delegation to meet with company officials. Pullman refused. Debs offered to submit the dispute to arbitration. Again Pullman refused. The delegates finally prevailed, and by June 28, 125,000 railroad workers had joined the boycott of any train hauling Pullman cars, tying up some 20 railroads.

The employers, through their General Managers Association, set out to break the strike by any means possible. They arranged to have Pullman cars attached to virtually all trains, especially mail trains, so that the strikers might be provoked into "interfering with the U.S. mail" despite ARU instructions to keep the mail trains running. At the request of U.S. Attorney General Richard Olney (a former railroad corporation lawyer), President Grover Cleveland sent federal troops to Chicago on Independence Day, July 4, 1894. The day before, a sweeping federal injunction forbidding any and all strike activity had been granted to the railroads (the ARU was not even notified of the hearing). Ironically, the injunction had been granted under the provisions of the Sherman Anti-Trust Act, which had been passed in 1890 to curb the power of giant corporate combinations such as Pullman and the railroads.

Dozens of agents provocateurs had been hired by Pullman and the railroads to stir up violence among the strikers. On July 7, federal troops opened fire on a crowd protesting the movement of a wrecking train in Chicago, killing an estimated 30 persons. That same day, Debs and other strike leaders were arrested for conspiracy and posted bond. Ten days later, they were arrested again, this time for contempt of court, and jailed. With its leadership jailed, its treasury depleted, and its members blacklisted on virtually every railroad, the ARU was finally broken.[3] Gompers and the AFL had declined assistance, even to counter the newspaper propaganda of the Managers Association. The Pullman workers stayed out until fall, but they were finally starved into submission.

Elsewhere and for the next 25 years, the story was much the same, eventually even for the AFL. Employers in the metal trades formed a Metal Trades Association to do battle with the Machinists. Chicago contractors completely eliminated union representation following a one-year strike in 1899. The National Founders Association successfully broke union contracts and work rules and

[3]During his six-month jail sentence, Debs read voraciously and became convinced that socialism was the only answer to the growing struggle between labor and capital. Upon his release, he became a leader of the Socialist Party and was its presidential candidate in 1900, 1904, 1908, 1912, and 1920, when he received nearly a million votes. In 1918, while speaking in defense of Socialists who had been arrested under the Espionage Act, he was himself arrested under the same law. After an unsuccessful appeal to the Supreme Court, he was sentenced to 10 years in federal prison. In 1920, the Socialist Party nominated Convict #9653 at Atlanta for President of the United States. While in prison, Debs polled over 900,000 votes.

Debs was one of the great orators of his time; he dared to speak out for unions as an indispensable part of a true democracy. His idealism and humanitarianism brought many new leaders into the labor movement. He maintained his commitment to workers until he died in 1926.

almost the Molders Union itself. In 1901, U.S. Steel broke 14 union contracts with the Amalgamated Association of Iron, Steel, and Tin Workers (AFL) after a three-month strike.

But from 1895 to 1920, the labor movement, dominated by a business union philosophy, managed to grow, reaching a membership of over 5 million by 1920—some 12 percent of the labor force. It was, however, an unbalanced and precarious quarter-century of growth, as evidenced by numerous tragic worker-employer confrontations. With the exception of the unions in mining, breweries, and the clothing industries, there was little place in the AFL for the unskilled American factory worker.

The call to organize industrially was again taken up in 1905 by the radically militant Industrial Workers of the World (IWW), or "Wobblies," as they were known, under the leadership of such colorful figures as "Big Bill" Haywood and the poet/songwriter/organizer Joe Hill. The Wobblies' initial strength was among metal miners and loggers in the West, but their high point of strength and victory came when they assumed leadership of a strike by unskilled textile workers in Lawrence, Mass., in 1912. After a bitter struggle, including violent police intervention, the Lawrence strike was won, with benefits extended, for a short time, to thousands of other New England textile workers. The following year, however, an equally bitter struggle on behalf of the Paterson, N.J., silk workers was lost, marking the beginning of the end for the Wobblies.

In the West, the United Mine Workers' organizing drives, led by such staunch and colorful figures as Mary "Mother" Jones, were finally crushed in 1914 after National Guard troops attacked an evicted miners' tent colony at Ludlow, Colo., on April 20, killing 5 men, 2 women, and 13 children. The copper barons in Utah likewise resorted to harsh actions, eventually, it is alleged by many historians, framing Joe Hill on a murder charge. He was executed on November 19, 1915.

The Wobblies' radical approach to union organizing was not particularly enticing to industrial workers at the time, but their support of an organization which openly advocated the overthrow of capitalism demonstrated the desperation of unorganized workers across the country. But just as the Wobblies appeared about to become a union of unskilled and semiskilled workers rivaling the AFL, World War I provided increasingly nervous employers with a rationale for using the powers of government to crush the IWW on the basis of its opposition to U.S. involvement in the war.

In June 1917, the Federal Government indicted the entire top leadership of the IWW under the wartime espionage laws. IWW publications were suppressed, union halls raided and shut down, and the organization harassed and prosecuted into virtual extinction. There can be no doubt that the so-called "Red scare" was used, if not planned, by employers to rid themselves of the growing union threat, whether IWW, AFL, or otherwise. Progressive leadership in unions such as the Fur and Leather Workers, the Amalgamated Clothing Workers, and the International Ladies' Garment Workers was attacked along with that of the IWW. The high point of hysteria was reached on the evening of January 2, 1920, when agents of U.S. Attorney General A. Mitchell Palmer, and his special assistant J. Edgar Hoover, arrested some 10,000 persons, including numerous labor leaders, across the country, many of whom were held for days or weeks without bail pending deportation as "alien opponents of the United States Government."

Labor's Wartime Prosperity and Postwar Repression

The AFL had grown rapidly from 1917 to 1920 during the war and the months of prosperity following it. Its membership doubled from 2 million to 4 million, and represented more than 80 percent of all union members. Wartime conditions had created a tight labor market, giving unions considerable bargaining power. Most important to AFL growth, however, was the Wilson Administration's grant of organizing and collective bargaining rights free of employer discrimination in return for Gompers' and the AFL's pledge of no strikes and full cooperation with the war effort. Under Wilson's policy of "new freedoms," organized labor for the first time in American history was brought into the councils of government. The combination of war and a friendly administration was good for unions—at least for the AFL at the time.

Real wages increased more than 20 percent during the war, but with the cessation of hostilities and a return to peacetime economic conditions that soon resulted in postwar recession and depression, employers decided to turn back the clock to the "good old (nonunion) days." The deportation of more than 50 Wobblies and the arrests of thousands during the Palmer raids were only two signs of the crackdown that had been building for some time.

Labor had been buoyed by wartime gains in bargaining strength. Significantly, 1919 represented an all-time high in the percentage of workers involved in strikes. Particularly notable were a general strike in Seattle, a police strike in Boston, and major strikes in steel and coal—the former lost after five months by the 24 AFL unions claiming jurisdiction in the steel industry, the latter halted after 10 days by a permanent federal injunction. The employers were obviously ready and waiting and were aided by the courts, which granted injunctions and other antiunion rulings.

The Clayton Act, passed in 1914 and hailed as "labor's Magna Carta" by Samuel Gompers for its exemption of unions from antitrust laws (the Sherman Act) and injunctions, suddenly became labor's nemesis. The Supreme Court denied the validity of labor's exemption under the Clayton Act in 1921 and then proceeded, in 1922 and 1923, to strike down child labor and minimum wage statutes as violations of the "freedom of contract." Antilabor injunctions began to flow more freely than ever before.

By far the most significant contribution to decline and stagnation in the labor movement during the 1920s was a massive nationwide open shop drive by major corporations and the National Association of Manufacturers. This drive was facilitated by the apparent indifference of the AFL, under the leadership of its new president, William Green (Gompers died in 1924 after having headed the AFL for all but one of its first 38 years), to the changed structure of American industry and the increasing number of industrial workers. The "Red scare" was used to fan the flames of superpatriotism in the Roaring Twenties. Under the slogan "American Plan," unions were portrayed as not having the best interests of America at heart.

As a substitute for genuine worker control, companies established their own brand of "welfare capitalism." Some set up elaborate employee benefit programs for recreation, health care, and even profit sharing, appearing to offer workers a voice in their wages, hours, and working conditions. But in actuality only an advisory voice was given workers. If they had a union, it was often a "company union," where management decided what could be negotiated as well as the final terms and conditions of employment.

At the time of the stock market crash in October 1929, organized labor was considerably smaller and weaker than it had been 10 years earlier. By 1930, membership had fallen to 3.6 million, a 28-percent decrease from its 1920 high. By 1933 and the depth of the Great Depression, membership stood at less than 3 million, just barely above that of 1916, prior to World War I.

Depression, Reform, and Challenge From the CIO

It was by far the worst depression in the nation's history. Between 1929 and 1933, the gross national product fell from $104 billion to $56 billion, a drop of nearly 50 percent, while unemployment increased from 3.2 percent to nearly 25 percent of the civilian labor force. But the AFL remained opposed to social security, unemployment compensation, and minimum wage legislation, claiming that these measures represented unnecessary and unwanted government intervention. And despite the fact that increasing numbers of union activists were by then supporters of the Democratic Party, the AFL, as usual, endorsed neither candidate in the 1932 Presidential election.

The election of Franklin Delano Roosevelt ushered in a tide of economic and social legislation designed to save a desperately sick capitalist economy. In fact, prior to the New Deal, the bubble of optimism over the infallibility of American economic institutions had burst. In 1932, the Norris-LaGuardia Act severely limited the conditions under which injunctions could be issued in labor disputes and outlawed the infamous yellow-dog contract, which, by allowing employers to force nonunionism as a condition of employment, had long been used against labor, especially in the coalfields.

The first important piece of labor legislation passed under the Roosevelt Administration was the National Industrial Recovery Act (NIRA), which specifically granted workers the right to organize unions and bargain with their employers through representatives of their own choosing. From the time of its passage in mid-1933 until it was declared unconstitutional by the Supreme Court in early 1935, well over 1 million rank-and-file workers in mass production industries organized themselves, formed locals, and applied directly to the AFL for charters. And AFL national unions reorganized many of the craft locals that had been lost in the previous 15 years.

Within the AFL, however, there remained sharp and increasing divisions over what to do with the millions of industrial workers clamoring for union organization. As a temporary solution, the AFL accepted new locals of industrial workers as directly affiliated local unions. The sentiment among a growing number of AFL leaders, led by John L. Lewis of the United Mine Workers, Sidney Hillman of the Amalgamated Clothing Workers, and David Dubinsky of the International Ladies' Garment Workers, was that the federation must change its policies toward organizing in mass production. If the labor movement was to grow and meet the challenges of the depression and beyond, they thought, the AFL would have to charter national unions on an industry basis—in steel, auto, glass, electrical, and the like.

The final confrontation came at the 1935 AFL convention when the craft unionists narrowly prevailed, refusing to allow unions composed of what Teamster president Daniel Tobin described as "rubbish" mass production workers. Lewis then established the Committee for Industrial Organization (CIO), made up of AFL unions in favor of organizing in mass production industries. Lewis hoped that the AFL would change its mind, but Green and the AFL executive council were furious over this sin of so-called "dual unionism." They expelled all 10 AFL national union members of the CIO in August 1936.

The passage of the National Labor Relations Act (Wagner Act) in 1935 gave workers even stronger protections than they had had under the NIRA. The Wagner Act placed an outright ban on company unions, provided for secret-ballot representation elections, and established the National Labor Relations Board (NLRB) to administer and enforce the Act's provisions, which included a specific enumeration of employer unfair labor practices against which the Board would issue citations to violating employers.

With the law solidly behind it and millions of industrial workers obviously waiting for and wanting union representation, the CIO, which changed its name to the Congress of Industrial Organizations in 1938, began the most remarkable organizing drive in the nation's history. By 1941, with the nation still floundering in depression, the CIO unions had some 5 million members, and virtually all of the giant industrial corporations were under CIO affiliate union contracts. Spurred by the success (or more aptly, the competition) of the CIO, the AFL abandoned its craft orientation and began organizing industrially itself, with major campaigns in meatpacking, paper, electrical, auto, and other industries.

At the time of Pearl Harbor (December 7, 1941), total union membership stood at over 10 million, more than a threefold increase in just eight years. For the first time in history, the American labor movement, even though divided (AFL and CIO), was a powerful economic and political force representing the broad spectrum of workers—skilled, semiskilled, and unskilled; craft and industrial. But the victories had not come easily or without bloodshed. Many employers had continued their flagrant violation of the Wagner Act, hoping that it would soon be overturned in the courts as the NIRA had been. The Supreme Court upheld the constitutionality of the NLRA in 1937, but on May 30 of that year, Chicago police opened fire on a peaceful demonstration of organizing Republic Steel employees and their families, killing 10 and injuring scores in the infamous "Memorial Day massacre." It took sitdown strikes in Akron and Flint before rubber and auto companies agreed to accept union representation. The events in Akron, Detroit, and Chicago were repeated in many other cities in the 1930s and early 1940s. Thousands of new leaders gave their lives, many literally, to the union cause.

Unions in a War and Postwar Economy

As had been true during World War I, labor made great advances during the Second World War, in large part due to joint labor-management promises to support the war effort. The AFL and the CIO together were given equal representation on the War Labor Board, which handled collective bargaining disputes during the war years 1942–1945. By the end of the war, total union membership (AFL, CIO, and independent) was 14.5 million, representing an all-time high of 35.8 percent of the labor force. But the labor movement, which had grown by over 40 percent in just four years, was soon to fall on hard times due to a combination of events that brought its rapid growth to a standstill and for a time (1948–1950) caused membership to actually fall.

For the most part, the war years were free of open labor-management conflict. Notable exceptions occurred in the auto industry, where the United Auto Workers faced continuing opposition from Ford, which had not been organized until 1941, and in coal, where Lewis defied the law by conducting major industrywide strikes, challenging the power of the President and the War Labor Board. Immediately after the war, however, the floodgates of pent-up worker demands were opened; inflation prompted unions to flex their newly attained collective bargaining muscles. In 1946, there were nearly 5,000 work stoppages, involving over 4.5 million workers. Bitter strikes occurred in virtually every major industry, including steel, railroads, auto, and coal. As a result, there was growing public dissatisfaction (most often at the instigation of employer groups and sensationalized by the news media) with what were considered union abuses of power.

In 1947, the newly elected, Republican-controlled Eightieth Congress passed the antilabor Taft-Hartley Act (Labor Management Relations Act) over the veto of President Harry Truman. Taft-Hartley severely limited or revoked many rights previously granted under the Wagner Act. In particular, the Act enlarged the legal realm for issuing injunctions, outlawed mass picketing, enumerated unfair labor practices for which unions could be enjoined (and sued), denied unions the right to contribute to federal political campaigns, outlawed the closed shop, and prohibited secondary boycotts. And as an extra attraction to employers, for whom New York Representative Donald O'Toole said the bill had been written "page by page, by the National Association of Manufacturers," Section 14 (b) allowed individual states to outlaw the union shop and other types of union security clauses, creating so-called "right-to-work" states.

In addition to Taft-Hartley, which was and continues to be a severe handicap to union growth, the labor movement in the post-war period was subjected to the "Red-baiting" hysteria of the cold war McCarthy era. In 1949 and 1950, the CIO expelled 11 of its own national unions on accusations of Communist domination, costing the federation an estimated one-half million members and further splitting the unity of the labor movement, as both the AFL and the CIO sought to enroll the members of the ousted unions. In the early 1950s, the wave of anti-Communist fanaticism became so great that all unions were once again attacked as patently un-American. The mood was typified by an Akron *Beacon Journal* editorial which concluded, "Actually a union doesn't need to be communist-dominated or to be led by communists to constitute a potential danger to industrial society."

A lasting consequence of the period's domestic and international turmoil was that organized labor, overall, became more conservative in its policies and programs. It is widely agreed that by the mid 1950s there was no longer a strong left inside the labor movement to debate and counter forces of the right.[4]

Jurisdictional disputes as well as attacks by employers had placed a severe strain on union treasuries. Both the AFL and the CIO were aware that their competition was not only counterproductive but also contributed to the environment for passage of antilabor legislation such as Taft-Hartley. The deaths, only 11 days apart in 1952, of AFL and CIO antagonist chieftains William Green and

[4]For a detailed account, see David Caute, *The Great Fear: The Anti-Communist Purge Under Truman and Eisenhower*, especially Part Five, "Pacification of the Working Class." New York: Simon and Schuster, 1978, pp. 349–403.

Philip Murray removed another barrier to merger of the two federations.

Late in 1954, George Meany, the new AFL president, and Walter Reuther, head of the CIO, announced that after nearly two years of preliminary discussion and negotiations, the AFL and the CIO would become a single federation, the American Federation of Labor-Congress of Industrial Organizations. The agreement, signed on February 5, 1955, created the 16.1-million-member AFL-CIO with Meany as president and William Schnitzler (AFL) as secretary-treasurer.[5]

Principal among the founding tenets of the AFL-CIO was the acceptance of each national union as an autonomous body, in deference to AFL concern that many of its smaller affiliates would be absorbed by larger CIO unions. An Industrial Union Department, with Reuther as president and James Carey of the International Union of Electrical Workers (CIO) as secretary-treasurer, confirmed the structural pluralism of the new federation; that is, of organization by trade *and* industry. In addition, the extension of no-raiding pacts that had been negotiated between rival unions prior to the merger was encouraged along with the voluntary consolidation of competing organizations.

Beyond the Merger

There were sounds of alarm in corporate America during the mid-to-late 1950s that the AFL-CIO would expand its membership rapidly and begin a new period of growth in power and influence. But for a variety of reasons, and to the disappointment of many unionists who hoped the corporations were for once correct in their views, there was no great expansion. One reason was that in spite of the merger and official calls for unity, deep philosophical differences remained that frustrated organization and service activities. It was in part these conflicts which prompted the United Auto Workers to eventually withdraw its 1.4 million members in 1968 and become an independent union.

Another reason for AFL-CIO stagnation was increasing concern and publicity over corruption and racketeering in some unions.

[5]In Canada in 1956, the Trades and Labor Council (TLC) and the Canadian Congress of Labor (CCL) merged to form the Canadian Labor Congress (CLC). The CLC, with which most U.S. unions with Canadian members are affiliated, has the same basic structure and functions as the AFL-CIO in the United States (see Chapter 4).

Merger is symbolized at the first AFL-CIO convention in 1955 by George Meany (left), president of the former AFL and new president of the newly merged organization, and Walter Reuther, president of the former CIO.

AFL-CIO Information Department

In 1957, the International Brotherhood of Teamsters, the Laundry Workers, and the Bakery and Confectionery Workers were expelled for alleged domination by "corrupt influences." These expulsions occurred following congressional investigations leading to the 1959 passage of the Landrum-Griffin Act (Labor Management Reporting and Disclosure Act), which in part amended the Wagner and Taft-Hartley Acts. In particular, the Landrum-Griffin Act guarantees union members a "bill of rights" for their democratic protection and establishes strict procedures for the management of union funds.

But perhaps most contributory to postmerger stagnation in the labor movement were two factors over which labor remained relatively powerless. First were the effects of Taft-Hartley legislation, especially its so-called "right-to-work" (open shop) provisions and the increasing use of the courts and other legal maneuverings by employers to resist union organization, particularly in the southern United States, where much of the postwar industrial development had taken place. Second was the rapidly changing nature of employment. Well into the 1960s, the tremendous increase in white-collar and service employment relative to blue-collar manufacturing employment had created, along with a more affluent, middle-class society, worker-employer relationships that were less easily aligned with the laboring-class philosophy of the pre-AFL-CIO labor movement of the 1930s and 1940s. Despite significant union gains among white-collar and service workers, especially in the public sector (federal, state, and local government), organizing was hampered by social and employer-fostered attitudes implying that "professional" workers should not join unions. In addition, relatively few public employees had the same rights of organizing and collective bargaining as workers in the private sector, covered by Wagner and Taft-Hartley legislation.

The expulsion of the Teamsters and the withdrawal of the United Auto Workers caused membership of unions affiliated with the AFL-CIO to fall by more than 2 million from 1955 to 1970. To say that organized labor as a social, political, and economic force ceased to exist, however, could hardly be further from the truth.

Most of the "Great Society" and other progressive legislation of the 1960s almost certainly would not have received congressional approval, at least in the form it did, had it not been for the tireless efforts of union lobbyists both in and out of the AFL-CIO. Labor support was crucial to the passage of such far-reaching laws as the Manpower Development and Training Act of 1962, the Equal Pay

Act of 1963, the Civil Rights Act of 1964, the Economic Opportunity Act of 1968, the Age Discrimination in Employment Act of 1968, and the Coal Mine Health and Safety Act of 1969. In addition, labor support was critical to improvements in existing social welfare legislation such as minimum wage and social security.

A middle ground of success and failure was demonstrated by labor's difficulty in purging itself of restrictive racial policies, in spite of internal reforms and its overall and important support of civil rights and equal employment opportunity legislation. On the darker side of organized labor's image and activity during the 1960s was the official AFL-CIO support of U.S. involvement in Vietnam in the face of growing opposition from other social/welfare organizations, including individual national unions. (Opposition to AFL-CIO foreign policy positions was another major reason for the United Auto Workers' withdrawal in 1968.)

Apart from its mixed contribution in resolving controversial political issues, labor continued to make advances on the collective bargaining front during the 1960s. In particular, Executive Order 10988, issued by President John Kennedy in 1962, granted strong organizing but limited bargaining rights to Federal Government employees. November 1964 marked a successful end to four and one-half years of dispute over work rules between the railroads and five major unions. The mid-1960s saw increased efforts toward coalition bargaining by different unions having contracts with the same company and increased organizing among public and professional employees (in particular by the American Federation of Teachers and the American Federation of State, County, and Municipal Employees). In 1966, the AFL-CIO chartered the United Farm Workers Organizing Committee, led by Cesar Chavez; the following year, it created the AFL-CIO Council of Scientific, Professional, and Cultural Employees to foster cooperation among affiliate unions organizing and serving workers in these rapidly growing fields of employment.

For the most part, labor held its own through the 1970s. Major organizing victories were won in the vineyards of California, the Virginia coast shipyards, and auto plants in the South. New union organizations such as the Coalition of Labor Union Women (1974), the International Union of Police Associations, and Professional Athletes Association (1979) were chartered; and consolidation continued through a growing number of mergers, notably among the unions of railway, postal, paper, printing, and retail workers.

Legislative gains included passage of the Occupational Safety

The founding convention of the Coalition of Labor Union Women.

UAW Solidarity Magazine/Archives

and Health Act (1970) and the Employee Retirement Income Security Act (1974). Also in the 1970s, labor increasingly took its message to the public—for example, through the creation of the Citizens/Labor Energy Coalition (1978) and initiating numerous consumer boycotts including those of J. P. Stevens, Farah, Coors, and Winn-Dixie.

But postmerger stagnation turned into out-and-out decline by the early 1980s. The worsening legal and organizing climates of the 1950s and 1960s had been compounded by increasing internationalization of the economy beginning in the 1970s. American corporations as a whole became more and more global in their efforts to maintain markets and profit margins. Hundreds of thousands of jobs in such heavily unionized industries as auto, steel, and apparel were "exported" as companies transplanted their operations in Third World economies. Further membership losses resulted in these and other basic industries due to the incursion of foreign-based, nonunion multinationals. And finally, the recession of 1981–1982 turned out still more organized workers, many of whom were not recalled during the recovery as their jobs had been replaced by automation and streamlined labor requirements.

For those still working, one result was greatly increased competition over wages and working conditions--not only among U.S. workers but even more so between them and their counterparts in other, less-developed countries. A most startling consequence of this turn in economic events is that the United States, for the first time in its history, is now experiencing what portends to be a long-term if not permanent shrinking of its middle class.

Adding to the woes of the labor movement in the 1980s have been numerous other antiunion developments. For example, a wave of deregulation has cracked previous union strongholds in the airline and interstate trucking industries, leaving the established (organized) companies and their workers vulnerable to new, nonunion firms. Also, corporations have implemented a variety of "innovative" measures to escape unionized workforces, such as "double breasting" whereby a company establishes a nonunion subsidiary to bleed work from its unionized operations. This practice is particularly prevalent in the construction and trucking industries.

The economic growth that has taken place in the last 10–15 years has occurred, for the most part, in regions and industries outside the traditional domain of the U.S. labor movement. The Sun Belt (largely "right-to-work" states) population has grown six times as fast as in the Great Lakes and New England regions. And about

90 percent of all new jobs have been created in the service sector, less than 10 percent of which is represented by organized labor.

Labor had begun to react before this most recent deluge. In the late 1970s, its retrenchment and consolidation included a number of significant steps including the mergers already mentioned and UAW reaffiliation with the national AFL-CIO. Another promising concerted effort was the Progressive Alliance of the UAW, the Machinists, and the State, County and Municipal Employees, for the advancement of a labor political agenda. However, like the Teamster/UAW/Chemical Worker Alliance for Labor Action a decade earlier, this venture foundered and failed as its member unions became distracted by their own specific problems.

Labor's troubled state became most evident with a dramatic turn of events in the summer of 1981. Contract negotiations between the Professional Air Traffic Controllers Organization (PATCO) and the federal government had reached an impasse. Although forbidden by law from striking, PATCO gambled, that since other federal unions such as the Postal Workers had struck with minimal retaliation from the government, and because it was one of the few unions to endorse President Reagan in the 1980 general election, it too would face minor repercussions from a walkout. Also, candidate Reagan, in seeking PATCO support, had assured the union of his sympathies for issues over which the union eventually struck.

But PATCO will be remembered in history as having misjudged both the man and the times. "In view of labor's appalled high command," wrote A. H. Raskin, "the Reagan thrust represented the most naked exercise of presidential power to crush a union since Grover Cleveland" broke the Debs-led Pullman strike in 1894, by ordering federal troops to move the mails.[6] The PATCO disaster clearly marked the dawn of a new, stark era for labor; one that would require new strategies and tactics for growth, let alone survival.

As suggested in the beginning of this chapter and as will be discussed in subsequent chapters, especially Chapter 7, the issues and problems of the American and world labor movements are the result of at least 200 years of trial and error, success and failure. With this exposition of the determining influences of history behind

[6]"Unions in Reaganland" *The New Yorker*, Vol. LVII, #29, September 7, 1981, page 50.

us, we turn now to a review of important legal considerations that have likewise helped shape the nature and course of labor relations as we know it today.

Review and Discussion Questions

1. What conditions led to the formation of the first local unions in America?
2. Why did "boom and bust" economic conditions throughout the nineteenth and early twentieth centuries have such a profound influence on union organization and growth?
3. What economic changes in the post-Civil War period led to increased pressures from workers for union organization?
4. Contrast the union philosophies of the Knights of Labor and the American Federation of Labor.
5. What do you think accounted for the longer-range success of the AFL compared to the Knights of Labor?
6. Why were employers so quick and vicious in their attempts to crush industrial unions such as the Knights of Labor, the American Railway Union, and the Industrial Workers of the World while paying relatively less attention to the American Federation of Labor and its member unions?
7. Why did rapid growth of industrial unions in the United States not begin until the mid-1930s? Why did it not continue after the Second World War?
8. Why was the AFL as a whole opposed to organizing workers industrially? Was the CIO equally opposed to craft unions?
9. Contrast the social, political, and economic backgrounds of the Wagner Act and the Taft-Hartley Act.
10. What were the principal causes of relatively slow union growth in the 25-year post-World War II period? And what conditions were most responsible for this slow growth turning into outright decline by the 1980s?
11. Which of the theories of union development and behavior discussed in Chapter 1 can you match, in whole or in part, to particular union organizations mentioned in this chapter?

Key Words and Phrases

AFL-CIO
agent provocateur
Alliance for Labor Action
American Federation of Labor
American Plan
arbitration
autonomous national union
blacklist
blue-collar employees
boycott
Canadian Labor Congress (CLC)
capitalist exploitation
central body
Citizens/Labor Energy Coalition
Clayton Act
closed shop
Coalition of Labor Union Women
Committee for Industrial Organization
Commonwealth v. *Hunt*
company union
compulsory arbitration
Congress of Industrial Organizations
consumer boycott
cordwainer doctrine
corporate capitalism
court injunction
craft guilds
craft union
directly affiliated local union
dual unionism
economic depression
economic strike
Employee Retirement Income Security Act
employer association
exclusive unionism
Executive Order 10988
factory union
general strike
Great Depression
Great Society
inclusive unionism
industrial union
Industrial Workers of the World
internationalization of the economy
injunction
international union
job action
Labor Management Relations Act
Labor Management Reporting and Disclosure Act
Landrum-Griffin Act
less-developed countries
lockout
mandatory bargaining
means test
Memorial Day massacre
multinationals
National Industrial Recovery Act
National Labor Relations Act
National Labor Relations Board
national union
New Deal
no-raiding pact
no-strike clause
Norris-LaGuardia Act
Occupational Safety and Health Act
open shop
Palmer raids
PATCO
Progressive Alliance
real wages
"Red-baiting"
"Red scare"
restraint of trade
"right-to-work" state
"scab"
secondary boycott
Sherman Anti-Trust Act
sitdown strike
strike
strikebreaker
structural pluralism
sympathy strike
Taft-Hartley Act
unfair labor practice
union recognition
union security clause
union shop
wage labor
Wagner Act
War Labor Board
welfare capitalism
white-collar employees
Wobblies
worker/producer cooperative

Chapter Resources and Suggested Further Reading

Complete bibliographical information for the following titles can be found in the Bibliography.

Boyer and Morais, *Labor's Untold Story.*
Brooks, *Toil and Trouble: A History of American Labor.*
Butler, *Labor Economics and Institutions.*
Montgomery, *Workers Control in America.*
Sloane and Witney, *Labor Relations.*

General history of American labor unions:

Fillipelli, *Labor in the USA: A History.*
Raybeck, *A History of American Labor.*
Uhlman, *American Trade Unionism—Past and Present.*
U.S. Department of Labor, Bureau of Labor Statistics, *Brief History of the American Labor Movement.*

Contrasting historical perspectives:

Foner, *History of the Labor Movement in the United States. Vols. I and II* (left-political analysis).
Taft, *Organized Labor in American History* (traditional work).
Zinn, *A People's History of the United States.*

Period accounts:

Caute, *The Great Fear: The Anti-Communist Purge Under Truman and Eisenhower.*
Galenson, *The CIO Challenge to the AFL: A History of the American Labor Movement, 1935–1941.*
Josephson, *The Robber Barons: The Great American Capitalists, 1881–1901.*
Laslett, *Labor and the Left: A Study of Socialist and Radical Influences in the American Labor Movement, 1881–1924.*
Pierson, *Unions in Postwar America.*
Taft, *The AF of L in the Time of Gompers.*

Black and women workers:

Fuentes and Ehrenreich, *Women in the Global Factory.*
Marshall, *The Negro and Organized Labor.*
Wertheimer, *We Were There: The Story of Working Women in America.*

Illustrated histories:

Cahn, *A Pictorial History of American Labor.*

Morris, *The American Worker.*
Schnapper, *American Labor, A Pictorial Social History.*

The great companies did not know that the line between hunger and anger is a thin line.

—John Steinbeck, 1939

3

The Legal Framework of Labor-Management Relations*

I admit being opposed to the present system. I am doing what little I can, and have been for many years, to bring about a change that shall do away with the rule of the great body of the people by a relatively small group and establish in this country an industrial and social democracy.

—Eugene V. Debs, 1918

As discussed in Chapters 1 and 2, prior to industrialization, workers seldom faced situations calling for collective action. In an agricultural and small shop/craft economy, workers usually were either self-employed (owned their own tools) or slaves or indentured servants. Trade unions in the modern sense of concerted action by workers to improve their wages and working conditions could only develop under a wage-labor system, where workers must sell their labor power to employers. In this context, workers realized that they could improve their wages and working conditions by dealing collectively with employers (the buyers of their labors). Individually they were powerless, forced by economic reality to compete with each other in terms of the wages and conditions they would accept.

From the birth of the trade union movement in the United States, public law, particularly as developed and applied by the courts, has been an important force shaping labor-management relations. Until the 1930s, the law was generally unfavorable toward workers combining to protect their self-interest. Early law reflected

*Betty Justice, an attorney and union advocate from Foster, West Virginia, contributed much of the original material for this chapter. Her skills and effort are gratefully acknowledged.

classical economic theory, in which free operation of the "laws" of supply and demand was considered essential. According to this theory, control of wage rates by workers artificially inflated prices, ultimately harming commerce, the community, and even workers themselves, because higher prices discouraged consumption and created unemployment. Therefore, according to many observers, the best prescription for a healthy economy was one free of either government regulation or private regulation via collective action of workers.

Until 1935, application of these restrictive theories of law inherited from England reflected the political assumption that free competition and the sanctity of contract and property rights of individuals were fundamental values of society that must be protected. Since 1935, labor-management relations in the United States have been subject to comprehensive government regulation with the stated purpose of protecting the public interest in the stability and free flow of commerce. Although this regulation initially helped unions to flourish, it has served since 1947 to channel disputes into narrow legalistic categories, undercutting efforts of workers and unions to become more conscious of their interests as a group vis-à-vis employers as a group.

Regulation by the Courts

Initially, U.S. employers sought with the aid of the courts to suppress unions entirely, through the use of the criminal conspiracy doctrine.[1] Until 1842, the mere act of joining together to affect wages and working conditions was considered a criminal conspiracy. For such activity, union members could be prosecuted in the same manner as someone accused of robbery. The fact that such activity was considered a crime meant that it was viewed as interfering not only with the rights of the employers but with society's interest as well. As the judge observed in the first U.S. conspiracy prosecution, "A combination of workmen to raise their wages may be considered in a two-fold point of view: one is to benefit themselves . . . the other is to injure those who do not join their society. The rule of the law condemns both." (*Commonwealth v. Pullis,* Philadelphia cordwainers, Pennsylvania, 1806).

[1]A conspiracy is a combination of two or more persons who join together to impede the rights of others or of society. No overt act needs to take place in order for accused conspirators to be found guilty.

As greater numbers of workers recognized the need to join together to protect their interests, in spite of the fact that such an act was considered a crime, it soon became evident that workers' organizations could not be totally suppressed. The first major break in the conspiracy (cordwainer) doctrine occurred when, in *Commonwealth v. Hunt* (Massachusetts, 1842), the Supreme Court of Massachusetts held that the simple act of joining a union was not a crime. Instead, the court applied a "means test," under which the methods used by a union, as well as the ends it sought to achieve, were considered in deciding whether concerted worker activity was legal.

Using this test, courts continued to cripple workers' efforts to further their collective interests. However, criminal law was replaced by civil law,[2] particularly the use of civil injunctions, by the 1880s. An injunction is a remedy known in the law as an "equitable remedy." It is based on a concept in early English law in which the Chancellor of Equity was empowered to issue orders to achieve fairness regardless of the legalities of a situation. An injunction is issued to maintain the status quo until legal issues can be decided and to prevent irreparable harm to another party's rights.

An injunction must be obeyed as long as it is in effect regardless of the circumstances under which it was granted. In labor disputes it matters little what the merits of a situation are, since the mere granting of the injunction is usually sufficient to constrain the activity enjoined.

Because injunctive power is intended to achieve fairness, none of the protections present in "legal" proceedings, such as the right to a jury or, in some cases, the right to appear and object to the issuance of the order, applies. Violation of an injunction is punishable not only because the enjoined party continues to violate the rights of the party which obtained the injunction, but also because the enjoined party has challenged the authority of the court. Therefore, a contempt fine or sentence is proper, even if an appeals court later decides that the injunction was not appropriately granted.

Any judge of general jurisdiction has the power to grant injunctions. Since employers could "shop around" until they found a sympathetic judge, injunctions were routinely available against any

[2]Civil law refers to a suit between two private parties or between the government and a private party over their respective rights. In a criminal matter, the government—representing the public interest—seeks to punish a party for illegal conduct.

combined worker activity that was allegedly carried out by illegal methods or sought to achieve illegal goals. The illegality of both methods and goals was determined by existing law, all of which was based on the sanctity of property and the right to contract. This law was, of course, highly unfavorable to workers, whose purpose in organizing was to diminish the absolute power employers possessed under the existing system.

By the latter part of the nineteenth century, the civil injunction had become the preferred legal method of combating labor organizations. Employers were almost always able to obtain injunctions against unions on some basis. The injunction, with its advantage of speed and flexibility, was even more effective than the criminal law had been in stifling unions. The reach of the injunction was virtually unlimited in the conduct that could be enjoined. It was less cumbersome than criminal prosecution, being both speedy and simple. Additionally, it avoided a hearing before a jury potentially sympathetic to workers and their organizations. Its use in labor disputes was held constitutional by the Supreme Court in the *Debs* case (1895), which arose out of the Pullman strike by the American Railway Union in 1894.

The full force of the injunction was felt in its use to enforce "yellow-dog contracts." When it became clear that the Supreme Court revered the "freedom to contract," employers were encouraged to use yellow-dog contracts as yet another, and very effective, way to prevent worker organization." Whenever a union attempted to organize workers covered by these contracts, the employer would seek an order enjoining the union (particularly union organizers) from interfering with them. The propriety of injunctions in such situations was specifically approved in *Hitchman Coal & Coke v. Mitchell* (1917) and in subsequent cases when the Supreme Court overturned state laws that outlawed yellow-dog contracts. The yellow-dog contract used by the Hitchman Coal and Coke Company read in part:

> I am employed by and work for the Hitchman Coal and Coke Company with the express understanding that I am not a member of the United Mine Workers of America, and will not become a member of the United Mine Workers of America so long as I am in the employ of the Hitchman Coal and Coke Company . . . and that the Hitchman Coal and Coke Company is run nonunion and agrees with me that it will run nonunion so long as I am in its employ. I have either read the above or heard same read.

Early Statutory Regulation Experience Under the Antitrust Laws

Prior to 1890, the law applied to labor organizations was strictly common law—law developed by judges without any guiding statutes[3] in the context of actual disputes brought to their attention. Since 1890, many laws have been enacted which affect the right of workers to organize. Today court decisions on labor matters are statutory interpretation rather than common law.

The Sherman Anti-Trust Act was passed by the Congress in 1890 to limit the ability of industry to engage in price fixing and other concerted acts that lessened competition. However, the impact of the law was more severe on unions than on employers and provided yet another basis for combating unions. The Sherman Act declared illegal "every contract, combination . . . or conspiracy in restraint of trade." It provided for criminal penalties and injunctions against violations and entitled anyone injured by unlawful conduct to sue for damages of three times the amount actually sustained. In the hands of an unfriendly Justice Department and federal court system, this law became another way to prevent organized labor's growth.

The application of the Sherman Act to unions was upheld by the Supreme Court in *Loewe v. Lawlor* (the Danbury hatters case, 1908), in which members of the United Hatters of America were sued for restraint of trade when they organized a nationwide boycott of stores selling hats produced by a nonunion firm. The union and its individual members were found liable for damages resulting from their secondary boycott. This decision was a crushing blow in that it outlawed one of labor's most effective organizing weapons, the secondary boycott, and discouraged workers from organizing for fear of the personal consequences of the union's "illegal" activity.

Another decision of the period reflected the depth of the hostility of the courts toward organized labor. The AFL had placed the Bucks Stove and Range Company on its "We Don't Patronize" list because of its refusal to recognize and bargain with the Molders and Foundry Workers Union. An injunction was obtained by the company against the AFL, and Samuel Gompers and other union officers were subsequently held in contempt of court and sentenced to jail because the AFL continued to include the company on the list.

[3]A statute is law made by a legislative body.

The contempt citations were overturned on a technical ground, but in a 1911 decision, the U.S. Supreme Court, reviewing the Gompers case, ruled that a boycott promoted by words and printed matter was indeed a violation of the Sherman Act.

In 1914, after intensive lobbying efforts by organized labor, Congress passed the Clayton Anti-Trust Act, which labor believed would exempt its organizations from the antitrust laws (Section 6) and limit the right of federal courts to issue injunctions in labor disputes (Section 20).

However, the Clayton Act was written in vague language and did not explicitly provide what labor hoped for—that is, an outright exemption. The Supreme Court was still unwilling to allow Congress to legislate away its role as the protector of the status quo. The Court in interpreting the Clayton Act (*Duplex Printing Co. v. Deering*, 1921) concluded that in view of the use of the terms "lawful" and "lawfully" and "peaceful" and "peacefully" in reference to union activities, Congress had intended to confer immunity only to activity that was permitted under the law at the time of the Clayton Act's passage. This meant that anything violative of the Sherman Act could not be protected under the Clayton Act—and thus the law changed nothing. The courts remained unhampered in their collusion with management to control worker organization. The Clayton Act did provide that private parties could seek injunctions in antitrust cases, whereas only the Government had been empowered to do so under the Sherman Act; so the law actually increased the power of employers to obtain injunctions against unions, further handicapping organizing efforts.

During the first quarter of the twentieth century, it became clear that the Supreme Court employed a double standard in its application of antitrust law to labor and business. The Court, in reviewing business combinations, distinguished between "reasonable" and "unreasonable" restraint of trade, finding that only the latter was unlawful. For instance, the organization of the U.S. Steel Corporation was found not to be a violation although it took place for the express purpose of acquiring the stock of independent companies and by 1920 gave U.S. Steel control of 50 percent of the nation's steel industry.

In contrast, the United Mine Workers were convicted in the *Coronado Coal* case (1925) when they struck a mine the company was attempting to run on a nonunion basis despite a current valid contract with the UMWA. The significance of *Coronado Coal* is that the union activity was directed at the employer immediately involved rather than at secondary parties, as in the Danbury hatters and Gompers cases. Since all strikes have the effect of reducing the amount of products in commerce, this decision cast doubt on the legality of any strike.

The double standard was most clearly revealed in the *Bedford Cut Stone* case (1927). It involved an employer association of 24 corporations operating in Indiana and producing 70 percent of all of the cut stone produced in the nation. These corporations had joined together to control the cut stone industry. In 1921, the association refused to extend its collective bargaining agreement, provoking the Journeyman Stonecutters Association to forbid its members to work on stone cut by nonunion workers. The Supreme Court held that the union's conduct violated the antitrust law because it prevented the use and installation of the association's products in other states and necessarily threatened to restrain interstate trade. The Court seemed to be saying that monopoly restraint of trade was "reasonable" but that workers' attempts to protect themselves from monopoly abuses were "unreasonable."

Railway Legislation

Because of the impact of railroad transportation on the public welfare, it is not surprising that the first efforts in developing a national labor policy focused on the railway industry. Several serious strikes occurred late in the nineteenth century, including the famous Pullman strike of 1894, which brought the western rail industry to a virtual standstill. Such conflicts provided the incentive for congressional actions designed to bring order to the chaotic labor relations of the industry.

The first of these actions was the (Arbitration) Act of 1888, which provided for voluntary arbitration of railway disputes. Other legislation, such as the Erdman Act of 1898, the Newlands Act of 1913, and the Adamson Act of 1916, was enacted over a 30-year period and gradually provided for greater direct government participation in the labor-management relations of the industry. A variety of issues were addressed, such as yellow-dog contracts, the eight-hour day, the right of workers to join unions, and a public board to consider and adjust labor-management disputes which could not be settled privately. The Supreme Court did not look altogether favorably on these efforts, finding, for example, that Section 10 of the

Erdman Act outlawing yellow-dog contracts was unconstitutional (*Adair v. United States*, 1921).

The Railway Labor Act of 1926 incorporated the more progressive aspects of earlier legislation and was supported by both the industry and the unions representing railroad workers.[4] The Act established the right of railroad workers to join unions and to select collective bargaining representatives without employer interference; it also established a joint labor-management obligation to bargain with each other. The Act did not establish a means of government enforcement of these rights, nor did it provide for penalties. Instead, it relied on negotiation between the private parties and on mediation and voluntary arbitration of unresolved differences. The constitutionality of the Railway Labor Act was upheld by the Supreme Court, when it expressly approved collective bargaining in the industry as promoting the public interest (*Texas & New Orleans Railroad v. Brotherhood of Railroad Clerks,* 1930). The Act has been amended several times to strengthen and clarify the right to organize and bargain collectively and to introduce penalties for its violation.

Today, because of economic similarities, the amended Railway Labor Act covers employees in the airline industry as well. Procedures for the selection of bargaining representatives, contract negotiations, dispute settlement, and Presidential intervention in emergency situations are very similar to those of the Wagner and Taft-Hartley Acts; in fact, much of the latter's form and content was drawn from the experience of railway labor legislation.

The Norris-LaGuardia Act

Finally, in 1932 Congress enacted the Norris-LaGuardia Act,[5] which in direct and clear language denied federal courts the right to issue injunctions in ordinary labor disputes. The Act also removed labor activities from the sanction of antitrust laws, outlawed the yellow-dog contract, and drastically limited the jurisdiction of federal courts in boycotts, picketing, and strikes.

Union liability aspects of the law were clearly stated in the Su-

[4]Many labor economists and historians feel that the industry came to accept unions as the lesser of two evils. The prospects for increasing government regulation, possibly even nationalization of the railroads, were strong enough at the time to encourage industry support for its own unionization.

[5]The Norris-LaGuardia Act was sponsored by Senators George Norris of Nebraska and Fiorello LaGuardia of New York.

preme Court *Apex Hosiery* (1940) and *Hutcheson* (1941) decisions, which virtually exempted unions from civil cases (suits for damage), criminal cases, and injunctions under the antitrust laws, so long as they act in "self-interest." *Apex Hosiery* and *Hutcheson* effectively overturned the *Coronado Coal* doctrine that all strikes were illegal, but in a 1945 decision, *Allen Bradley v. Local 3, IBEW*, the Supreme Court ruled that unions were not exempt from antitrust prosecution if they acted in collusion with a nonlabor group—in particular, their employer.

In passing the Norris-LaGuardia Act, Congress noted for the first time the general imbalance of power that had long existed between individual workers and their employers. (It had previously done so only with respect to railroad workers.) The Act spoke favorably on the development of unions and collective bargaining as a method of redressing inequalities.

Norris-LaGuardia can be attributed in part to labor's greater consciousness and exercise of its political power, but persons concerned with saving American capitalism were also influential in securing its passage. Working people had lost their respect for and faith in the federal courts as neutral parties in the settlement of industrial conflicts. The malfunctioning of the system that had brought on the Great Depression made it much easier for people to lose faith in other basic institutions. Restraining the federal courts' ability to impede labor's organizational efforts was a step toward recapturing that faith.

The preamble of the Norris-LaGuardia Act stated that law had long recognized and aided the right of capital to consolidate itself, which had rendered individual, unorganized workers helpless to exercise effectively their freedom of labor and liberty of contract in order to obtain acceptable terms and conditions of employment. Therefore, under Norris-LaGuardia, the law recognized the right of employees to have full freedom of association and self-organization and to designate representatives of their own choosing to negotiate terms and conditions of employment free from the interference, restraint, or coercion of employers.

The philosophical underpinning of the Norris-LaGuardia Act was the belief that government should not resolve labor disputes or substitute its determinations for private contracts in a free market. This policy of allowing labor and management to resolve their disputes without federal intervention lasted only three years, however, before the United States adopted the policy of comprehensive regulation that characterizes labor-management relations today.

The National Industrial Recovery Act

The New Deal's general plan to promote economic improvement was contained in the National Industrial Recovery Act (NIRA), adopted by Congress in 1933. It provided for the regulation of prices and production by the operators in an industry. This industrial self-regulation was an effort to rationalize the economy and represented an express departure from the antitrust laws. The NIRA further required that each covered industry establish a minimum wage for its workers. Section 7(a) of the Act provided the right of workers to organize and bargain collectively.

President Roosevelt created the National Labor Board (NLB) to administer the labor policy of the NIRA. But because of a lack of enforcement powers, the NLB was successful only when employers did not challenge its authority. Consequently, in 1934 Congress passed Joint Resolution No. 44, creating a board to enforce Section 7(a). Questions of enforcement soon became moot, however, because the Supreme Court declared the NIRA unconstitutional. The Court ruled in *Schecter v. United States* (1935) that the NIRA represented an attempt to regulate business transactions that were not part of interstate commerce.

The Wagner Act

The major statute regulating private industry labor-management relations in the United States was the Wagner Act, sponsored by Senator Robert Wagner of New York. The Wagner Act, formally called the National Labor Relations Act (NLRA), was passed by Congress in 1935 as part of the response to the deteriorating stability of the nation's industrial and commercial life. The NLRA represented the Government's first major legislative step into an arena previously regulated by the organized economic strength of the two parties. Of course, the Government had long been involved via the courts, maintaining all the while that the judiciary was not regulating labor-management relations but was simply enforcing other legally protected rights.

Abandoning altogether the remnants of the laissez-faire philosophy calling for government neutrality with respect to economic enterprise, Congress in the Wagner Act declared that the policy of the United States was to encourage the practice of collective bargaining and full freedom of worker self-organization. The law placed the full power of the Federal Government behind trade unionism.

A common belief is that Congress passed the Wagner Act *solely* because workers needed unions. However, the policy statements of both the original law and, later, its Taft-Hartley amendments clearly show that another purpose was the "free and full flow of commerce." Stated otherwise, the need for industrial stability prompted Congress to recognize the legitimacy of unions. It was hoped that unions, by countering the power of employers, could bring order and stability to the otherwise unrestrained and chaotic practices of businesses. That Congress chose to empower unions with this responsibility rather than to impose industrial order by direct governmental action reflected the prevailing ideology abhorring government intrusion into business. The vitality of that notion has persisted even to the present day in the debates over the appropriateness of government regulation of such substantive aspects of employment as health and safety and discriminatory personnel policies.

Specifically, employees covered by the NLRA were guaranteed in Section 7 the right to organize through secret ballot elections and to bargain collectively.[6] To further assure realization of these rights, Section 8 of the Act prohibited five types of employer conduct, defined as "unfair labor practices":

(1) Interference with employee rights of self-organization;
(2) Domination of or interference with the formation and administration of unions;
(3) Discrimination to encourage or discourage union membership;
(4) Employee discrimination or discharge for filing unfair labor practice charges or giving testimony under the Act; and
(5) Refusal to bargain with the duly chosen representative of employees.

The responsibility for the enforcement of the law and overseeing the process by which employees were to select their collective bargaining representatives was vested in a newly created federal agency, the National Labor Relations Board. The NLRA survived a challenge to its existence when the Supreme Court ruled that it was within the commerce power of the Congress to regulate labor-man-

[6]The Wagner Act applied to most workers and employers in the private, profit-making sector of the economy. Specifically exempted from coverage as employers, however, were labor organizations, hospitals, and other "nonprofit" organizations. Employee exemptions included agricultural laborers, domestic servants, independent contractors, and workers covered by the Railway Labor Act.

agement activity in the public interest (*NLRB v. Jones & Laughlin Steel Corp.*, 1937).

The Taft-Hartley Act

In one sense, the NLRA was highly partisan in that it imposed restraints on employers but not on employees or unions. This preferential treatment was based in part on the fact that despite a high level of individual worker militance, unions as institutions were relatively weak. The NLRA was conducive to union organizing and the establishment of stable collective bargaining relationships and therefore allowed unions to flourish.

However, the Taft-Hartley Act,[7] adopted just 12 years later in 1947 and formally known as the Labor Management Relations Act (LMRA), began a period of regulation and restriction that continues unabated to the present day.

Conversion to a peacetime economy following World War II was accompanied by strikes in major industries. This activity formed the backdrop against which Congress passed the Taft-Hartley Act (actually a series of amendments to the Wagner Act). Taft-Hartley, today often cited as *the* federal labor law, represented a basic shift in the regulatory scheme from protecting unions to restraining them.

The Labor Management Relations Act, enacted over President Harry Truman's veto, was premised on the belief that unions were no longer fragile institutions that needed special protection. In fact, proponents of Taft-Hartley argued that overprotection had resulted in unions becoming so strong that they exercised a stranglehold over the economic life of the nation and tyrannical control over their members.

Section 7 of the NLRA was amended to include the right of employees to *refrain* from engaging in organizing and concerted activities. Closed shops were outlawed, states were empowered to enact so-called "right-to-work" laws that restrict the application of union security agreements, various union practices were prohibited as secondary boycotts, and the NLRB was empowered to seek injunctions against such activity. Unions were made subject to unfair labor practice charges paralleling those applying to employers. Additionally, the LMRA guaranteed employers a "free speech" right

[7]The Taft-Hartley Act was introduced by Senator Robert A. Taft of Ohio and Representative Fred A. Hartley, Jr., of New Jersey.

to express their opinions concerning unions, provided for national emergency injunctions against otherwise legal contract strikes, and made labor contracts enforceable in federal courts.

The Landrum-Griffin Act

During the 1950s, much public attention was focused on corruption and the lack of democracy in the internal operations of unions, particularly the Teamsters. Not coincidentally, the Teamsters had been very successful in securing wage and benefits gains for their members and, as the largest and one of the most powerful unions in the country, was a natural target of those who wanted to keep labor in line. The result was the adoption of the Labor Management Reporting and Disclosure Act (LMRDA) of 1959, popularly known as the Landrum-Griffin Act.[8]

The Labor Management Reporting and Disclosure Act contains elaborate reporting requirements, particularly on the handling of money, designed to cure the problem of corruption. The LMRDA created a union member's "bill of rights" in such matters as union meetings, elections, eligibility for office, and union disciplinary proceedings. It also amended the National Labor Relations Act to clarify and close loopholes in the secondary boycott provisions, further restricting the range of legal union activity.

Of the Landrum-Griffin amendments, Titles I, IV, and V are most important to the rank-and-file union member. Title I contains the "bill of rights," which, among other things, gives every member an equal right to attend, participate in, and vote on the business of union meetings, and to nominate candidates and vote in union elections. It protects freedom of assembly and speech regarding union affairs and sets protective standards for disciplining union members, allowing individual members to sue their union for violation of Title I rights provided that they have first exhausted internal union appeal procedures.

Title IV of the LMRDA regulates union elections, specifically protecting the rights of candidates challenging incumbents, and allows the U.S. Department of Labor, upon petition, to bring suit to set aside an election if it concludes that the outcome was affected by improper conduct.

Title V requires union officers to conduct themselves as trust-

[8]The Landrum-Griffin Act was introduced by Representatives Philip Landrum of Georgia and Robert Griffin of Michigan.

ees of the membership and to refrain from activities of self-interest. Originally this title was meant to protect the membership's financial interests, but it has more recently been interpreted to cover all of the activities of union officers.

Collective Bargaining in the Public Sector

Executive Order 10988, issued by President John Kennedy in January 1962, granted agency employees of the executive branch of government (Cabinet departments and the Post Office) organizational and bargaining rights essentially the same as those of workers in the private sector.[9] The major difference between Executive Order 10988 and the Taft-Hartley Act was a prohibition of the right to strike and of arbitration of any kind over impasses in contract negotiations. Additionally, only arbitration of an *advisory* nature was permitted in grievance procedures. Binding arbitration was expressly forbidden. Finally, the scope of permissible bargaining issues was more limited than in the private sector; for example, agency budgets, the assignment of personnel, technological changes (automation), and salaries and wages set by congressional act were removed from the bargaining arena. Nonetheless, by 1970, 1.4 million federal employees (more than half) were represented by unions in 35 different agencies.

In January 1970, Executive Order 11491 made several changes and improvements in the law covering labor-management relations in the federal service. The order created a Federal Labor Relations Council to oversee collective bargaining in the Federal Government, much the same as the NLRB does under Taft-Hartley. In deference to the Landrum-Griffin Act, Executive Order 11491 required unions representing government employees to follow basically the same election, bonding, and financial reporting procedures required of unions in the private sector. An important feature of this order was the creation of a Federal Impasse Panel empowered to take any action deemed necessary to settle disputes over contract negotiations. The order also provided for limited final and binding arbitration in grievance disputes. These latter two changes corrected areas of substantial weakness in Executive Order 10988.

The Civil Service Reform Act of 1978 included a section (Title VII) consolidating federal labor-management relations law to date.

[9]Postal workers are now covered by the Postal Reorganization Act of 1970 which places them basically under the NLRA except for union security, impasse provisions, and the legal right to strike.

Essentially, Title VII codified the provisions of the two previous Executive Orders, making them less subject to revision or repeal, and gave a strong legal basis and independence to the Council, now called the Federal Labor Relations Authority (FLRA). However, Reagan appointees to the FLRA, like their counterparts on the NLRB, have more often acted to reverse previous union gains. By the mid-1980s, federal sector unions had begun considering alternative ways, such as informational picketing and new legislation, to resolve many of their problems.

Lacking the legal rights and protection extended to federal employees, except in a minority of states, non-federal government workers face even more difficult problems. With states and municipalities facing severe cuts in federal funding, their workers, despite the relative strength of their unions, have been confronted by a wave of austerity measures. At present, only a handful of states, all in the North, have meaningful public employee collective bargaining laws. The problem for most state and municipal workers is not that they are prohibited from joining unions; that issue was finally resolved in 1969 when the federal courts ruled that union membership was a right of association for which public employees are protected under the First and Fourteenth Amendments to the Constitution. The problem is simply that, as in the private sector before the Wagner Act, public employers in most states can refuse to recognize and bargain with the representatives of their employees.

In many states, there is increasing public support for granting municipal and state government workers meaningful collective bargaining rights, usually up to but not including the right to strike.[12] The "right-to-work" states have apparently not yet fully accepted these principles, even for private-sector employees.

In spite of extreme adversity, however, public employee unions, especially in the federal sector and in states with comprehensive labor laws, have grown faster than those in any other part of the economy. This growth has occurred despite a virtually universal prohibition of the right to strike and an almost equally widespread refusal of public employers to agree to third-party final and binding arbitration of either contract or grievance disputes.

[12]As of 1985, 42 states plus the District of Columbia and the Virgin Islands had some form of public employee labor legislation. Fifteen states had passed comprehensive laws covering all public employees—Florida, Hawaii, Iowa, Maine, Massachusetts, Minnesota, Nebraska, New Hampshire, New Jersey, New York, Ohio, Oregon, Pennsylvania, South Dakota, and Vermont.

Important Protective Labor Legislation

Labor law can logically be divided into two functional categories: *enabling* legislation, such as that contained in the Wagner and Civil Service Reform Acts which facilitate or "enable" unions to exist and operate as they do; and *protective* legislation, which is designed to enhance more specific aspects of the work environment. Obviously, some legislation deals simultaneously with both enabling and protective aspects of the law; for example, Title I of the Landrum-Griffin Act is intended both to facilitate and to protect the democratic rights of union members.

A brief review of the numerous protective laws is in order, since they are important determinants of the scope of labor-management relations. Historically, protective labor legislation has had a profound impact on the course and content of collective bargaining in American society. There is probably no better example of this impact than that of wage and hour laws. Prior to the passage of the federal Fair Labor Standards Act (FLSA) in 1938, most employers were free to pay as low a wage as they could. Approximately one third of the states had passed minimum wage laws prior to the 1930s, but these protected relatively few workers. The Davis-Bacon Act, adopted in 1931, required that minimum *prevailing* wage rates be paid to craft workers by contractors engaged on federal construction projects. In 1936, the Walsh-Healy Act established similar procedures for federal nonconstruction contracts in excess of $10,000.

The Fair Labor Standards Act, or wage and hour law, as it is commonly known, was originally an antidepression measure aimed at spreading work by requiring the payment of time and a half for all hours in excess of 40 hours per week and by eliminating child labor (thus creating jobs for adults). It was designed to prevent a worsening of the recession of 1938 by placing a floor of 25 cents per hour under wages "without substantially curtailing employment." Largely because of its distrust of government intervention, the AFL had long been opposed to minimum wage legislation except for women and children, but overall union experience with the FLSA very quickly proved favorable. Union support of minimum wage legislation not only benefited low-wage, unorganized workers but also created pressures for raising wages that were already above the minimum for more highly skilled and organized workers. The impact of minimum wage legislation on collective bargaining was and continues to be substantial.

Unemployment compensation is another protective law whose

origin dates back to the 1930s and the New Deal. Many supporters of the concept hoped that unemployment compensation would become part of the Social Security Act of 1935; but business interests prevailed, and states were encouraged through federal assistance and tax reduction credits for their industries to pass individual laws, thus creating the current array of vastly differing benefits among the states. In spite of the obvious refusal of many states to pay adequate unemployment benefits, which would eliminate incentives to accept low-paying employment, it must be remembered that much of the federal intent for unemployment compensation was to maintain purchasing power in the economy; this objective was viewed as being equal in importance to that of protecting workers from the adversities of joblessness. Unemployment compensation can thus be considered at least partially pro-business legislation.

The same can be said about compensating workers for financial and other hardships as a result of industrial accident or death. Early laws holding employers financially responsible for the injury or death of their workers were declared unconstitutional, but after the Federal Government passed injury compensation laws in 1908 for its employees, numerous states followed suit. Wisconsin was the first, followed by 29 others by 1915, and the Supreme Court finally upheld the constitutionality of these laws in 1917.[10]

Much of the change in attitude toward this form of protective legislation stemmed from the realization by businesses that they too could benefit, especially when states could establish their own laws and levels of compensation. Those businesses with the worst injury/death records pay the highest premiums, adding an element of fairness to the insurance program. Most critical to business acceptance of the concept of workers' compensation, however, was the realization that, by making government compensation the sole remedy available to an injured worker, business is relieved of total financial responsibility. Workers or their survivors can no longer sue for damages as a result of industrial injury or death. For employers, the financial obligations for industrial accidents has become a predictable and relatively fixed cost of doing business.

Several more recent examples of protective labor legislation should be mentioned. First is the Equal Pay Act of 1963, which prohibited wage differentials based on sex after June 10, 1964, for workers covered by the Fair Labor Standards Act. Although consid-

[10]Mississippi did not pass such a law until 1949, which underlines the problem of leaving protective legislation to individual states.

erable sex-based wage discrimination still exists, the Equal Pay Act has tended to have a beneficial impact on both organized and unorganized workers.

Title VII of the Civil Rights Act of 1964 contains major provisions protecting the rights of workers regarding their wages, terms, conditions, and privileges of employment. Specifically, workers are protected in these matters from discrimination on the basis of race, color, religion, sex, or national origin. In contrast to the procedural requirements of the Landrum-Griffin Act, Title VII ensures that a worker does not have to exhaust internal union procedures before going to court. In fact, even if a worker has lost a Title VII case through the grievance procedure (including arbitration), it is still permissible to go to court, because Congress considered the right not to be discriminated against to be more important than many other rights.

The Equal Employment Opportunity Act in 1972 and 1973 amended Title VII of the Civil Rights Act, further expanding government powers against discrimination in employment. In particular, Title VII coverage was extended to educational institutions and to state and local government. In addition, antidiscrimination protection was given to applicants for employment or union membership, bringing apprenticeship and other job training programs specifically under the law.

The Vocational Rehabilitation Act of 1972 provided important protection to disabled workers. The U.S. Department of Labor, in administering the Act, has interpreted its provisions to prohibit discrimination against workers with such disabilities as cancer, heart disease, and back problems. As a result, employers are no longer free to discharge disabled workers at will when the workers are most in need of employment and financial security.

The Occupational Safety and health Act (OSHA) of 1970 and the Employee Retirement Income Security Act (ERISA) of 1974 were both major additions to the arsenal of protective legislation for workers. As with the Coal Mine Health and Safety Act of 1969, after which many of its provisions were patterned, the first 10 years of OSHA advanced the interests of workers in securing their right to safe and healthy jobs. Indeed, even for the first few years of the Reagan Administration, occupational death and injury rates continued to decline. But, as documented by the Congressional Office of Technology Assessment in 1985, the Reagan-era agency cutbacks and easing of health and safety standards "effectively curtailed an already weak regulatory effort." By 1984, the rollbacks began tak-

Three hundred fifty ton punch press, circa 1940.

UAW Solidarity Magazine/Standard Oil Company (N.J.)

Occupational Safety and Health Act was passed in 1970.

ing their toll as workplace fatalities jumped 21 percent and injuries increased 13 percent over the previous year.

Despite Administration resistance—for example, workplace inspections were reduced by one third during Reagan's first term—the potential for OSHA effectiveness remains. It is possible to get a good OSHA inspection; and the recently promulgated (1986) Hazard Communication Standard, though not as stringent or wide in scope as many had hoped, may still have a major impact on controlling chemicals in the workplace.

One important benefit of OSHA has been its role in creating greater public awareness about workplace safety. The 1979 Schweiker bill, which would have permanently restricted OSHA enforcement, was defeated in part because of grass roots lobbying. Recent local initiatives for workplace and community "right-to-know" legislation (considered to be more effective than federal standards for alerting workers of hazardous materials) have grown out of health and safety education efforts begun by OSHA in the late 1970s. Another benefit has been renewed attention to safety and health issues in collective bargaining, where organized workers may still have their best chance to effect significant changes in this most important aspect of their work.

After decades of abuse at the hands of companies and pension program administrators, workers finally gained significant protection of their rights under employee benefit plans with the passage of the Employee Retirement Income Security Act. The 1974 Pension Reform Act, as ERISA is commonly known, set forth mandatory rules for pension plan participation. It also established rigid fiduciary rules, provision for financial audits, and, most important, standards for vesting of employee financial rights. The Pension Benefit Guaranty Corporation (PBGC) was created to insure plans against failure. In recent years, though, ERISA has been abused by corporations seeking to ease their own financial problems. By 1986, more than 1,000 companies had dumped their pension obligations on the PBGC. In 1985 alone, the agency's debt doubled to $1.3 billion when Allis-Chalmers and Wheeling Pittsburgh Steel unloaded their programs. The improper use of ERISA as a bailout tactic for mismanaged corporations has been compounded by Reagan Administration proposals to turn the mechanisms for guaranteeing pension plans over to private insurance companies. Industry executives and actuaries doubt the feasibility of these proposals. They fear that relying on the private sector to insure pensions will increase the possibility that many of the 30 million workers now covered by ERISA could lose their protection. And as if the message wasn't already clear enough, the President's Council of Economic Advisors argued in 1985 that underfunded pension plans were a good way to keep union wage demands in check.

Labor Law Interpretation: Some Important Court Decisions

As a prelude to our concluding discussion of labor law, a review of some representative and important court decisions is in order. This section covers three topics: the union as exclusive representative, the duty of fair representation, and labor law at the state level. A further discussion of the law of collective bargaining (contract negotiations) and contract enforcement by arbitration is contained in Chapters 5 and 6, respectively.

The Union as Exclusive Representative

A primary feature of U.S. labor law is the principle of exclusive representation by a majority union. This principle is specifically declared in Section 9 of the National Labor Relations Act, which states:

> Representatives designated or selected for the purposes of collective bargaining by the majority of the employees in a unit appropriate for such purposes, shall be the exclusive representative of all the employees in the unit for the purpose of collective bargaining in respect to rates of pay, wages, hours of employment, or other conditions of employment. . . .

This provision means that once a union is selected as the collective bargaining representative, by law it acquires the right *and* the responsibility to deal with the employer on behalf of *all* employees in the unit. This is true regardless of the possible desires of individual employees to represent themselves and regardless of whether or not employees are union members.

The National Labor Relations Act makes it an unfair labor practice for an employer to refuse to bargain collectively with the representatives of his employees. An employer is obligated to deal with a designated majority union and is forbidden by law to deal individually with employees or with a competing organization in regard to any matter subject to collective bargaining.

The primacy of the exclusive representation principle rejects any form of plural representation—either by individuals or by organizations other than the union. The justification for this doctrine is the belief that, in the long run, plural representation would allow an employer to foster rivalries among subgroups, thereby depriving employees of an effective united voice in asserting their interests.

An equally important aspect of exclusive representation is the channeling of all disputes into narrowly defined procedures, thereby insulating the employer from more basic challenges to its authority. This relieves the employer of the burden of dealing with individual employees who might be more militant in their demands than the union, which is severely restrained by both the law and the contract in its ability to assert employee interests.

The Duty of Fair Representation

A judicially developed corollary of a union's exclusive right to represent the members of a bargaining unit is its obligation to represent them fairly. Under the law, a union chosen by a majority enjoys the sole and exclusive authority to act on behalf of all of the workers in a bargaining unit whether or not they support the union, and employers are prohibited from negotiating with individual employees.[11] Therefore, the Supreme Court has read into the law a duty to represent fairly and fully the interests of all members of a unit for which a union holds representation rights. This duty of fair representation applies to all functions performed by a union on behalf of the members of a bargaining unit, specifically including negotiating contracts and processing grievances.

The duty of fair representation does not prevent a union from taking actions which may have a differential or even an unfavorable impact on some members. A union can permissibly exercise discretion in making its decisions even when those decisions draw distinctions among groups of employees.

Although decisions made in accordance with contract proceedings are ordinarily final and binding and cannot be either reviewed or considered anew in any public forum, suits alleging a breach of the duty of fair representation are exceptions. In *Hines v. Anchor Motor Freight, Inc.* (1976), the Supreme Court allowed a suit against an employer despite the fact that the plaintiffs had lost their arbitration case on the same issues. The Court said that an em-

[11] See page 156 for discussion of the right of individual workers to present and bargain over grievances.

ployer cannot hide behind the "final and binding" clause if the contractual proceeding was seriously flawed by the union's failure to represent its members fairly. This of course requires that the employee attempting to go beyond the grievance procedure and sue an employer must sue the union as well, and must prove both a breach of the contract *and* a breach of the duty of fair representation.

In its major announcement as to the nature of the duty and the standard of representation which a union must provide (*Vaca v. Sipes,* 1967), the Supreme Court emphasized that a breach occurs when the representation is carried out in an arbitrary, discriminatory, or bad-faith manner. This language contemplates conduct more serious than simple mistakes, errors in judgment, or even negligence. In effect, it requires that unions fully consider matters on the basis of merit *before* making decisions. They must be able to defend their intentions as well as their actions.

Labor Law at the State Level

A number of factors, including antigovernment and antiregulation mania and a deepening economic crisis, make it unlikely that new federal statutory law specifically covering labor-management relations will be passed in the next few years. The result of inaction at the national level may well be additional antilabor involvement of state governments in labor disputes.

In fact, the basis for such a move was established by the 1978 Supreme Court decision in *Sears Roebuck & Co. v. San Diego District Council of Carpenters.* The rule prior to this case (the *Garmon* doctrine) held that state proceedings were totally preempted by NLRB jurisdiction when conduct was arguably covered by the unfair labor practice provisions of the National Labor Relations Act. The preemption doctrine in effect precluded states' involvement in a wide range of labor disputes.

Sears Roebuck involved a trespass action under California law. The Supreme Court found that the controversy which would have been considered in a trespass proceeding was not the same as that which would have been presented in an unfair labor practice proceeding. Therefore, the Court reasoned, no significant risk of interference with NLRA-protected conduct existed, and consequently preemption was not appropriate.

This decision is an open invitation to employers and prosecutors to apply state law to deter union activity and to state legislatures to create new laws to repress union activity. Thus, in the coming years, state laws are likely to play an increasing role in private sector labor relations.

The Concept of Evolving Labor Law

From the foregoing, it is obvious that even though basic statutory law has remained the same since 1947, unions in the 1980s exist in an entirely different legal environment from that of their predecessors.

Unions today are subject to what can be referred to as evolving labor law—the result of years of judicial and administrative (NLRB) interpretation of our basic labor relations statutes. There is every reason to believe that this process will continue, sometimes favoring the growth of unions and sometimes hindering it.

One determinant of the effect of labor law on unions is the strength of the organized labor movement relative to the total labor force. Another determinant is the degree of militancy with which rank-and-file workers accept or reject unfavorable legal actions taken against what they perceive as their rights. Both organized strength and militancy are related to current labor relations controversies, including recent campaigns for labor law reform and the increase in organizing activity among public employees at the state and local levels.

Of particular interest to workers and unions in the building and construction trades industries has been the debate over situs picketing. In 1947, Taft-Hartley amendments to the Wagner Act outlawing secondary boycotts raised the question of whether striking employees of one employer at a construction site could picket the whole site and thereby affect some or all of the other employers and their employees at the same site. The basic issue is whether the work of various subcontractors on a construction job is so interrelated that they should be considered a single employing unit with a common economic purpose.

In 1951, on appeal from the NLRB, the Supreme Court ruled in the *Denver Building Trades* case that picketing of an entire job site was indeed a violation of the secondary boycott provisions of Taft-Hartley, thus essentially outlawing picketing in the construction industry. Since 1951, Congress has considered many proposals to overturn the *Denver* decision by legalizing common situs picketing. But it was not until 1976 that any such law passed both Houses and was sent to the President for final approval. The Ford Administration had promoted such legislation, but at the last minute, the President vetoed the bill, prompting the wrath of the labor movement and the resignation of his Secretary of Labor, John Dunlop.

Controversy over the common situs issue continues. Those in favor of a common situs picketing bill claim that such legislation would only give construction workers the same organizational and picketing rights as industrial workers. They claim that the contractors on construction jobs are not truly separate employers—that is, unconcerned third parties who should be protected from secondary boycott actions. Opponents claim that legalizing situs picketing would increase the already considerable power of construction trades unions and would allow them to force employers to deal only with union labor, thus preventing nonunion workers from securing employment.

The most recent attempt to revise federal labor law on a comprehensive basis was the proposed Labor Law Reform Act of 1977. The ineffectiveness of existing labor law in dealing with employers who violate it impelled organized labor to seek amendments designed to bolster enforcement. The proposed changes were primarily of two types. One type would have eliminated the delays that attend NLRB elections to choose bargaining representatives. These delays invariably aid employers in eroding a union's majority and are a significant factor in union losses in representation elections. Another set of changes would have made penalties for violating the law more severe, thereby providing an incentive for employers to comply with the law.

The proposed reform contained no major structural changes in labor relations law and did not address the glaring antilabor provisions contained in the Taft-Hartley Act. Rather, it was geared toward achieving the basic intent of a law enacted more than 40 years ago. It prompted frenzied opposition from employers and their organizations. After passing the House of Representatives, the reforms were finally shelved because filibustering prevented their being considered by the Senate.

The Reagan Era: From Evolution to Chaos

To most union observers, the PATCO incident in 1981 confirmed the existence of a much broader assault on labor—one that greatly exceeded the bounds of previous judicial and administrative interpretation. A 1984 congressional report concluded that the current state of affairs was such that, "the law is neither protecting individuals who advocate unions, nor is it protecting—much less encouraging—the collective bargaining process."

Internal to the process, the NLRB under the Reagan Administration has been widely accused of having altered the substance of the law in a manner contrary to its objectives. Virtually all of the Reagan Board's unusually high number of policy reversals have favored management—on such important questions as an employer's right to interrogate workers about their union sentiments, denying employees the right to refrain from hazardous work, and an employer's ability to escape its contractual obligations by abandoning a unionized facility.

The Reagan Board has also been responsible for a marked decline in administrative efficiency. Delays in investigating and correcting violations of the law take their toll, usually on workers and unions. Time as well as the penalties are on the side of the employers. By 1985, for example, the average time to obtain a court-enforced remedy for an employer's unfair labor practice had increased to three years. Thus, while a fired union sympathizer might, after a number of years, be reinstated, the only sanction facing the employer is the payment of back wages—minus whatever income the worker earned in the meantime—and posting a notice promising not to do the same again.

By the mid-1980s, many union officers and representatives were strongly urging their members to avoid taking disputes to the NLRB if at all possible. Others were recommending that workers and unions would be better off if the federal laws were scrapped and labor-management relations returned to the "law of the jungle" that existed prior to passage of the Wagner Act in 1935.

The apparent breakdown in legal protection and enforcement from within the system has understandably brought with it heightened attacks from without. By the mid-1980s, the annual "sales" of union-busting consulting firms (accountants, lawyers, psychologists, etc.), whose business is to help employers fight organizing and collective bargaining, had grown to more than $500 million per year. Among the results, an estimated one in 20 workers who vote for unionization is fired, illegally and permanently. The margin of union victories in organizing campaigns has fallen to an all-time low—well under 50 percent. And for approximately one third of the workplaces that are successfully organized, the union is prevented from obtaining an initial contract.

The end of this most recent evolution, or counterrevolution, in labor law is at this writing nowhere in sight. Although the Reagan years represented a radical departure from previous government practices concerning labor law enforcement, the seeds of this latest turnaround were planted well before 1981. Remember, that even with a Democratic President and Congress, it was impossible in the late 1970s to pass the common situs and labor law reform bills. And that, especially after the 1984 presidential campaigns, there were few remaining outspoken supporters of labor.

But just as conditions have grown worse for the labor movement, there is also evidence that the counterrevolution may have gone too far. Aware that the rules of the game have been drastically altered, workers and unions are currently devising new strategies to reverse the current trend of corporate dominance. Given the present imbalance of power, the labor movement has its work cut out for it.

Key Words and Phrases

Adamson Act
(Arbitration) Act of 1888
civil law
Civil Service Reform Act
classical economic theory
common law
contempt of court
criminal conspiracy doctrine
criminal law
Davis-Bacon Act
duty of fair representation
enabling legislation
Equal Employment Opportunity Act
Erdman Act
evolving labor law
exclusive representation
Executive Order 11491
express no-strike clause
Fair Labor Standards Act
Federal Labor Relations Authority
filibuster
final and binding arbitration
freedom of association
Garmon doctrine
Hazard Communication Standard
implied no-strike clause
Joint Resolution No. 44
Labor Law Reform Act of 1977
laissez-faire
legal strike
minimum wage
National Labor Board
Newlands Act
Pension Benefit Guaranty Corporation
plural representation
prevailing wage
protective legislation
Railway Labor Act
rank and file
refusal to bargain
representation election
right to engage in concerted activity
statutory law
sympathy strike
unemployment compensation
union officers as trustees
vesting of pension rights
wage and hour law
wage-labor system
Walsh-Healy Act
wildcat strike
workers' compensation laws
worker self-organization

Review and Discussion Questions

1. How were early conspiracy doctrines used to restrict union activity?

2. Discuss the significance of *Commonwealth v. Hunt* (1842).

3. What is an injunction? Historically, how were injunctions used to impede labor organization?

4. Why were the Danbury hatters, *Duplex Printing*, and *Coronado*

Coal cases important to the development of labor law? Briefly state the background and decision in each case.

5. How were the circumstances (in question 4) changed by the *Apex Hosiery*, *Hutcheson*, and *Allen Bradley* decisions?

6. The Railway Labor Act (1926) played a more significant role in the development of national labor law than most people realize. What was the significance of this legislation?

7. What were the key provisions of the Norris-LaGuardia Act?

8. What were the basic differences between the Wagner Act and the Taft-Hartley Act in their approaches to union organizing and collective bargaining?

9. What areas of union activity are covered by the Labor Management Reporting and Disclosure Act?

10. Describe and discuss the difference between enabling and protective labor legislation, and give examples of each.

11. What are the main economic and social justifications for unemployment and workers' injury compensation laws?

12. In terms of an enabling legal framework, what would you recommend to improve the organizing and bargaining environment of public employees at the state and local levels?

13. Describe and discuss the concept of evolving labor law mentioned in this chapter.

14. Review and discuss the principal arguments for and against legalizing common situs picketing.

15. Why do you think the courts have been so firm and unyielding in their interpretation and protection of the right of exclusive representation?

16. Describe and discuss the legal concept of the duty of fair representation.

Chapter Resources and Suggested Further Reading

Complete bibliographical information for the following titles can be found in the Bibliography.

Bloom and Northrup, *Economics of Labor Relations.*

Getman, *Labor Relations: Law, Practice, and Policy.*

Gorman, *Basic Text on Labor Law: Unionization and Collective Bargaining.*

Sloane and Witney, *Labor Relations.*

Smith, Merrifield, and St. Antoine, *Labor Relations Law*, 4th Ed. and Supplement.

Summers and Wellington, *Labor Law: Cases and Materials.*

Taylor and Witney, *Labor Relations Law.*

Whittaker, *The Common Situs Picketing Issue: Background and Activity in the 94th Congress.*

Legal framework of labor relations:

Anderson, *Primer of Labor Relations*, 21st Ed.
Justice, *Unions, Workers, and the Law.*
Lester, "Public Policy," in *Economics of Labor*, Part III.
Lynd, *Labor Law for the Rank and Filer* (pocket-size guide).
Morris, *The Developing Labor Law*, with Supplements.
Naffziger and Knauss, *A Basic Guide to Federal Labor Law.*
Tierney and Tucker, *Workers' Guide to Labor Law.*

Public sector labor law and union organization:

Economics Education Project, *Crisis in the Public Sector.*
Levine and Hagburg, *Public Sector Labor Relations.*

The labor of a human being is not a commodity or article of commerce.
—Section VI, The Clayton Antitrust Act, 1914

Experience has proved that protection by law of the right of employees to organize and bargain collectively safeguards commerce by removing certain recognized sources of industrial strife and unrest, by encouraging practices fundamental to the friendly adjustment of industrial disputes arising out of differences as to wages, hours, or other working conditions, and by restoring equality of bargaining power between employers and employees.
—Section I, National Labor Relations Act, 1935

Long ago we stated the reason for labor organizations. We said that they were organized out of the necessities of the situation: that a single employee was helpless in dealing with an employer; that he was dependent ordinarily on his daily wage for the maintenance of himself and his family; that if the employer refused to pay him the wages that he thought fair, he was nevertheless unable to leave the employ and resist arbitrary and unfair treatment; that union was essential to give laborers opportunity to deal on an equality with their employer.

—Chief Justice Charles Evans Hughes,
upholding the constitutionality
of the Wagner Act, *Jones &*
Laughlin Steel Corp. (1937)

4

Structure and Functions of the Labor Movement*

With all their faults, trade unions have done more for humanity than any other organization that ever existed. They have done more for decency, for honesty, for education, for the developing of character, than any other association.

—Clarence Darrow, 1909

Mere numbers can be boring but there's probably no better way to demonstrate the sheer size and complexity of the contemporary American labor movement. In 1982, there were 216 national and international labor organizations in the United States with a combined membership of nearly 20 million. These organizations were responsible for some 150,000 collective bargaining agreements covering workers in more than 50,000 affiliated locals and chapters.

Manufacturing industries accounted for 6 million union members; nonmanufacturing (mainly mining, construction, transportation, trade, and services) another 12 million; and government (federal, state, and local) the remaining 2 million. The largest labor organizations, with membership exceeding 1 million, were the Teamsters, the National Education Association, the Steelworkers, the United Auto Workers, and the Food and Commercial Workers. Forty others reported memberships of between 100,000 and 1 million (see Table 1). At the opposite extreme were unions such as the Coopers, the Horse Shoers, and the Siderographers—all with memberships of less than 500. The average membership for all labor organizations was just over 90,000.

*This chapter is based largely on the writings of Bloom and Northrup; Shister; and various public and union documents. See Chapter Resources and Bibliography for specific references.

Table 1. Unions Reporting 100,000 Active Members or More, Including Canadian Members, 1982[1]

Organization	Members	Organization	Members
Teamsters (IBT) (Ind.)	1,800,000	Electrical Workers (IUE)	190,786
National Education Association (NEA) (Ind.)	1,641,354	Letter Carriers (NALC)	175,000
Steelworkers (USW)	1,200,000	Graphic Communication Workers (GCIU)	165,000
Auto Workers (UAW)	1,140,370	Painters (PAT)	165,000
Food and Commercial (UFCW)	1,079,213	Firefighters (IAFF)	162,792
State, County (AFSCME)	950,000	United Electrical Workers (UE) (Ind.)	162,000
Electrical (IBEW)	883,000	Nurses (ANA) (Ind.)	160,357
Service Employees (SEIU)	700,000	Police (FOP)	160,000
Carpenters (CJA)	679,000	Iron Workers (BSOIW)	155,587
Machinists (IAM)	655,221	Bakery, Tobacco (BCTW)	152,100
Communications Workers (CWA)	650,000	Classified School (AACSE) (Ind.)	150,000
Teachers (AFT)	573,644	Mine Workers (UMW) (Ind.)	150,000
Laborers (LIUNA)	450,442	Sheet Metal Workers (SMW)	144,000
Clothing and Textile Workers (ACTWU)	400,000	Railway Clerks (BRAC)	140,000
Hotel and Restaurant (HERE)	375,000	Oil, Chemical Workers (OCAW)	125,000
Plumbers (PPF)	353,127	Bricklayers (BAC)	120,000
Operating Engineers (IUOE)	345,000	Transit Workers (ATU)	120,000
Ladies' Garment Workers (ILGWU)	276,000	Boilermakers (BBF)	117,642
Paperworkers (UPIU)	263,695	Longshoremen (ILA)	116,000
Musicians (AFM)	260,000	Transportation (UTU)	115,000
Retail (RWDSU)	250,000	Office and Professional (OPEIU)	112,793
Postal Workers (APWU)	248,000	Rubber Workers (URW)	100,175
Government Workers (AFGE)	210,000		

Source: Courtney D. Clifford, Directory of U.S. Labor Organizations, 1984-85 Edition, Washington, DC: The Bureau of National Affairs, Inc., 1984.
[1]All organizations not identified as (Ind.) are affiliated with the AFL-CIO.

Within 10 major industry classifications in 1980, unions accounted for 50 percent or more of the workers in primary metals, transportation equipment, the railroads, and the postal service. The least organized economic sectors included agriculture, banking, and private household service. Tables 2 and 3 show the distribution of organized workers by industry and state of residence in 1980.

Of the total eligible workforce (excluding supervisors and including nonmembers covered by collective bargaining agreements in "right-to-work" states), about one in three U.S. workers was represented by a labor organization in 1980, but by 1985 this ratio had fallen to around one in four. Still, the labor movement today is nearly 50 percent larger than it was at the end of World War II, despite the fact the organized portion of all workers has fallen over the last 40 years.

Our task in this chapter is to describe and explain, in brief, the

Table 2. Organized Employed Wage and Salary Workers by Industry, 1980.

(in thousands)

Industry	Organized Workers	Employed Workers	
		Number	Percent Organized
Agriculture	51	1,455	3.5
Mining	286	892	32.1
Construction	1,574	4,982	31.6
Manufacturing (total)	6,771	20,976	32.3
Durable Goods	4,366	12,546	34.8
Nondurable goods	2,405	8,430	28.5
Transportation, Communication, and Utilities	2,903	6,048	48.0
Retail and Wholesale Trade	1,753	17,401	10.1
Finance, Insurance, and Real Estate	190	5,152	3.7
Personal and Professional Services	4,743	26,121	18.9
Forestry and Fisheries	12	87	13.5
Public Administration	1,812	5,364	33.8
Postal	509	691	73.7
State	253	972	26.0
Local	703	1,906	36.9

Source: U.S. Dept. of Labor, Bureau of Labor Statistics.

Table 3. Labor Organization Membership by State and as a Proportion of Employees in Nonagricultural Employment, 1980.

(Membership in thousands)

State	Membership[1]		Total union membership[4] as a percent of employees in nonagricultural employment	
	1980	1980 rank	1980	1980 rank
All States	22,811	—	25.2	—
Alabama[2]	296	21	21.8	27
Alaska	57	46	33.7	6
Arizona[2]	160	30	16.0	39
Arkansas[2]	119	33	16.0	40
California	2,661	2	27.0	15
Colorado	227	27	18.1	32
Connecticut	327	18	23.0	24
Delaware	65	43	25.2	19
Florida[2]	420	16	11.8	47
Georgia[2]	323	19	15.1	44
Hawaii	113	36	28.0	13
Idaho	61	45	18.4	31
Illinois	1,487	4	30.4	8
Indiana	649	10	30.4	9
Iowa[2]	244	25	22.2	26
Kansas[2]	146	31	15.4	42
Kentucky	290	22	24.0	22
Louisiana[2]	257	24	16.4	37
Maine	101	37	24.1	21
Maryland-District of Columbia	527	14	22.8	25
Massachusetts	660	9	24.9	20
Michigan	1,289	6	37.3	2
Minnesota	463	15	26.2	16
Mississippi	135	32	16.2	38
Missouri	544	13	27.6	14

Montana	82	42	29.2	10
Nebraska[2]	114	34	18.1	33
Nevada[2]	95	39	23.8	23
New Hampshire	61	44	15.8	41
New Jersey	784	7	25.7	18
New Mexico	88	41	19.0	28
New York	2,792	1	38.8	1
North Carolina[2]	228	26	9.6	49
North Dakota[2]	42	47	17.1	36
Ohio	1,376	5	31.3	7
Oklahoma	174	29	15.3	43
Oregon	272	23	26.1	17
Pennsylvania	1,644	3	34.6	3
Rhode Island	113	35	28.3	12
South Carolina[2]	93	40	7.8	50
South Dakota[2]	35	50	14.8	46
Tennessee[2]	334	17	19.3	29
Texas[2]	669	8	11.4	48
Utah[2]	98	38	17.7	35
Vermont	36	49	18.0	34
Virginia[2]	318	20	15.0	45
Washington	553	12	34.4	4
West Virginia	222	28	34.4	5
Wisconsin	554	11	28.5	11
Wyoming[2]	39	48	18.9	30
Membership not classifiable[2]	376	—	—	—

Source: U.S. Dept. of Labor, Bureau of Labor Statistics.

[1]Based on reports from 125 national unions and estimates for 49. Also included are local unions directly affiliated with the AFL-CIO and members in single-firm and local unaffiliated unions.

[2]Has right-to-work law.

[3]Includes local unions directly affiliated with the AFL-CIO.

[4]Includes some retired members.

NOTE: Because of rounding, sums of individual items may not equal totals. Dashes indicate no data in category. Table is based on preliminary union survey structure and functions of present-day unions and the labor movement they comprise in this country. But before looking at the details of union organization and operation, it will be helpful to consider some of the principal determinants of the structure of American unions.

Structure of American Unions: Determining Influences

The various organizational and procedural relationships that exist among millions of workers, thousands of locals, and hundreds of international unions are very much the consequence of historical and legal developments discussed in the preceding chapters. For example, changes in technology that allowed employers increasingly to substitute unskilled and semiskilled production workers for skilled craft workers eventually forced the confrontation between the AFL and the CIO over industrial unionism. In the end, each federation recognized the indispensable role of the other in the growth and prosperity of the labor movement, thus prompting the structural pluralism of the AFL-CIO.

Changing technology and markets have also altered the organizing environment of both craft and industrial unions. Many crafts, including decorative plastering, carriage making, and wood lathing, have virtually disappeared, their workers replaced by machines or rendered unnecessary by new products. In the manufacturing sector, changes in products, markets, and technology have meant that industrial unions today must face multiplant and multiemployer bargaining, occupational health and safety, and many other issues that were vastly different or unknown only a few years ago.

A third determining influence on the structure of American unions and the labor movement has been the nation's legal history, especially in labor law. Section 7 of the National Labor Relations Act gives workers the right to organize and bargain collectively through representatives of their own choosing. Obviously, the law intended the choice of bargaining representatives to be a decision made by employees, not employers or union officials. In spite of and quite apart from internal agreements among unions as to their traditional organizing jurisdictions, workers are free to choose whatever union they desire. The old AFL principle of exclusive jurisdiction effectively died with the passage of the Wagner Act. The AFL-CIO merger confirmed the practice of worker choice of the unions to represent them. Thus while there are strict sanctions against AFL-CIO unions raiding the membership of other AFL-CIO unions, all are free to organize new workers, although the unions involved are expected to have had an historical interest in the craft or industry of the workers being solicited.

Although most workers choose a union familiar with and experienced in their particular line of work, there is a sound legal basis for many apparently incongruous bargaining units, such as the Ohio college whose employees are represented by the Electrical, Radio, and Machine Workers of America. In addition, in geographic areas where one union has traditionally represented many workers, others wanting union organization are likely to turn to a union that is familiar to them. Thus it is understandable, for example, to find many nonsteel Steelworkers' locals in Pennsylvania and many nonauto United Auto Workers' locals in Michigan.

Finally, both the structure and the functions of contemporary American unions have been shaped by the ebb and flow of historical currents. Personalities and politics have often been as critical to shaping the labor movement as technology and law. The American labor movement is in part a reflection of the personalities of Eugene Debs, Samuel Gompers, Mother Jones, John L. Lewis, George Meany, Walter Reuther, and William Sylvis as well as millions of working men and women.

It must be remembered as well that the politics of the labor movement reflects to a great extent the politics of the larger society of which it is a part. American society is competitive and profit-oriented, and in accepting, and even promoting, these characteristics, the labor movement has had to adapt itself accordingly. Its structure, as evidenced by autonomous international unions, collective bargaining, and active participation in the political arena, is geared toward working *within* the basic economic framework of capitalism, not toward opposing or altering it.

The increasing size and resources of unions in general have tended to produce bureaucratic and centralized organizational structures and functions similar to those in government and industry. But although many observers see an undesirable and increasing distance between union leadership and the rank and file, complicated by lingering problems of race and sex discrimination, the American labor movement as a whole remains one of the most highly democratic institutions in American society.

The remainder of this chapter will discuss the details of union democracy, in principle and practice, from the federation to the local union level; it concludes with a discussion of labor involvement in political education and action.

The Federated Labor Movement

Of the 216 labor organizations referred to in the beginning of this chapter, 95 were affiliated with the AFL-CIO in 1984. The total membership of AFL-CIO affiliates in that year was 13.8 million, or 70 percent of all union members. The majority of major international unions are AFL-CIO affiliates. Notable exceptions, which together account for about 80 percent of non-AFL-CIO union membership, are the Teamsters, the National Education Association, the United Electrical Workers, the Nurses, and the Mine Workers—of which all but the NEA and the Nurses were once AFL or CIO unions. The only other sizable international union never affiliated with either of the federations is the Brotherhood of Locomotive Engineers, whose membership was around 30,000 in 1982.

Organizational Structure of the AFL-CIO

The AFL-CIO is a *voluntary federation* of international unions. Its organizational structure closely resembles that of the former AFL. The chief members of the Federation are the international unions, the trade and industrial departments, state and local central bodies, and directly affiliated local unions (see Figure 1).

The supreme governing body of the AFL-CIO is its biennial convention; the voting strength of delegates is proportioned according to the per capita payments of member unions.[2] Convention proceedings include the election of officers and the consideration of constitutional amendments. Typically, however, most of the AFL-CIO convention is spent on committee reports and deliberations on internal policies as well as numerous resolutions on topics ranging from internal union affairs to U.S. Government domestic and foreign policy.

Between conventions, the two executive officers, assisted by the Executive Council and the General Board, direct the affairs of the Federation. The president of the AFL-CIO is its chief executive and has the authority to interpret the constitution between meetings of

[2]In 1985, AFL-CIO member unions paid 31 cents per month to the AFL-CIO for each eligible member.

New leadership of AFL-CIO elected at 1979 convention: Lane Kirkland (left), president, and Thomas R. Donohue, secretary-treasurer.

AFL-CIO Information Department

the Executive Council; he also directs the staff of the Federation. The secretary-treasurer is responsible for all financial matters.

The Executive Council is comprised of the two executive officers and 33 vice-presidents—by custom, selected from the presidents of the member international unions—elected by majority vote at the convention. The Council meets at least three times per year and has both promotional and administrative responsibilities, including proposing and evaluating legislation of interest to the labor movement; assisting organizing activity, which includes chartering new international unions; and hearing appeals in jurisdictional disputes among member unions.

The General Board consists of all 35 Executive Council members plus a principal officer of each affiliated international union and department.[3] The Board acts on matters referred to it by the executive officers or the Executive Council. Unlike the Council, whose votes are apportioned equally among members, Board votes are proportional—based on per capita payments to the Federation.

There are 13 constitutionally established Standing Committees of the Federation. They are representative of matters of interest to labor, such as legislation, civil rights, political education, community services, international affairs, and occupational health and safety. The committees carry out Federation policy and activities not specifically associated with a particular trade or industry.

Some of the Federation's staff departments perform the day-to-day business of the Federation (including accounting, data processing, and purchasing), while others have important and active ties to the various Standing Committees (in particular, community services, legislation, political education, research, and social security).

In the tradition of the AFL, the AFL-CIO departments deal with matters of craft or industrial interest to its affiliates. There are eight trade and industrial departments (see Figure 1), each of whose major function is to consider and act upon issues of concern to its affiliates, such as organizing, jurisdictional disputes, and legislation.

Member unions are allowed to affiliate with one or more departments; they pay per capita tax to each department on the individual members whose occupation comes under that department's jurisdiction. For example, the International Brotherhood of Boilermakers, Iron Ship Builders, Blacksmiths, Forgers, and Helpers

[3]Since its inception, the AFL-CIO General Board has seldom been used as a decision-making body within the Federation.

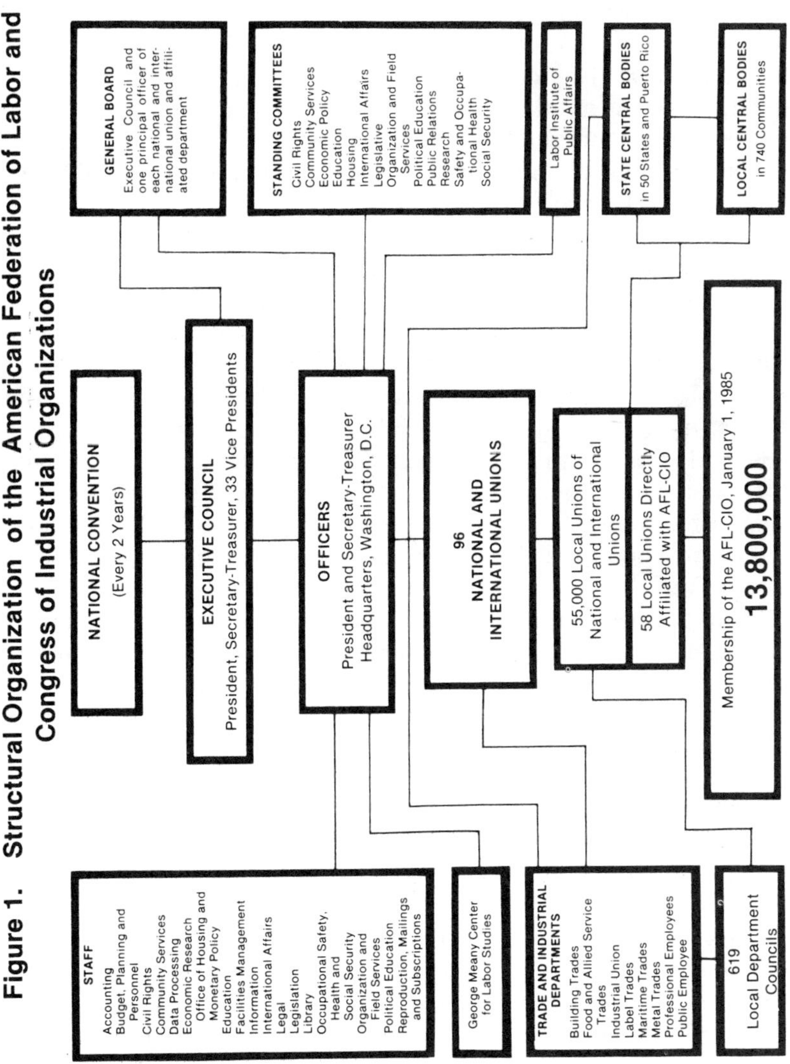

Figure 1. Structural Organization of the American Federation of Labor and Congress of Industrial Organizations

maintains membership in the Building and Construction Trades Department, the Industrial Union Department, the Maritime Trades Department, the Metal Trades Department, and the Railway Employees' Department, since it has members in all of these occupational groupings.

The Department of Organization and Field Services is organized and operates much differently from the trade and industrial departments. Most notably, it has no affiliated member unions. It is financed by the national headquarters and represents Federation interests through regional offices. The regional offices provide information and program activities in accordance with national Federation objectives.

The Federation also has established state and local central bodies to deal with problems at these levels. There are presently 51 state central bodies (including Puerto Rico) and 740 local central bodies, which are most often organized on a city- or county-wide basis. State and local central bodies are chartered directly by the national AFL-CIO, not by its member unions. The membership of these bodies is composed of local unions only (of internationals which belong to the Federation). Most AFL-CIO international unions urge their locals to affiliate with the appropriate state and local central bodies; some internationals require affiliation in their constitution.

The activities of state and local central bodies are similar, at their level, to those of the Federation. In particular, they do *not* engage in collective bargaining or regulate the internal affairs of their members. They *do* concentrate on issues of concern to their members, the labor movement, and workers in general, particularly through legislative and educational activities.

When the AFL and the CIO merged in 1955, directly affiliated local trade and federal labor unions (AFL) and local industrial unions (CIO) had a combined membership of 181,000. By 1984, the membership of local unions affiliated directly with the AFL-CIO had fallen to less than 10,000, in large part because many of the locals had affiliated with international unions over the years. It is likely that this trend will continue, eventually leaving very few directly affiliated locals as evidence of one period of American labor history.[4]

[4]A directly affiliated local union can send one delegate to the national AFL-CIO convention. Each AFL-CIO department and central body may also send one delegate.

Other Organizations

In addition to the AFL-CIO, three other associations or federations of unions operate in the United States. The Railway Labor Executives Association was founded shortly after the passage of the Railway Labor Act in 1926. The association functions as a coordinating and policy body in legislative and other areas of concern to railroad employees. Unlike the AFL-CIO, it does not intervene in jurisdictional disputes among its members, and its program is based entirely upon voluntary action. At present, the Railway Labor Executives Association is composed of the president of the Railway Employees' Department (AFL-CIO) plus a major official from each of the 19 international unions, all but one of which (the Locomotive Engineers) is affiliated with the AFL-CIO.

The Assembly of Government Employees (AGE) was founded in 1952 as the National Conference of Independent Public Employee Organizations. It is presently composed of 20 state, county, and local affiliated organizations and has a total membership of 250,000, mostly among state employees. AGE policies and programs are directed primarily at the establishment and maintenance of the merit principle, although its affiliates have considerable automony on specific work issues, including the use of the strike.

The National Federation of Independent Unions (NFIU) has 29 affiliates, with an estimated 60,000 members. As its name implies, the NFIU seeks to represent the interests of unions not a part of any other federation or, more often, any other international union. These unions are primarily confined to a single employer or locality.

The AFL-CIO and many independent unions are active in a number of multinational labor organizations which promote the interests of workers on a worldwide basis. The Federation has been especially involved in both the International Labor Organization (a tripartite body to whose conventions member nations can send four voting delegates—two from government and one each from labor and industry) and the International Confederation of Free Trade Unions (composed solely of labor organizations), although it has withdrawn its support from these and other international bodies at various times in protest of alleged Communist domination or leadership influence.[5] Additionally, the Federation contributes funds to

[5]After refraining from membership for several years, the United States rejoined the International Labor Organization (ILO) in 1980. The ILO is a specialized agency of the United Nations (UN).

aid in the organization of foreign workers, the training of foreign labor leaders, and other similar activities.

American unions also affiliate with numerous multinational trade secretariats, such as the International Chemical and Energy Workers Federation, the International Metalworkers Federation, and the International Transport Workers Federation. These federations function on a global basis, in much the same way as the various trade and industrial departments of the AFL-CIO.

Structure and Function of the International Union

International unions are the autonomous, self-governing units of the American labor movement. Even when an international union is affiliated with a federation such as the AFL-CIO, it retains the right to conduct its internal affairs and has considerable latitude with respect to outside activities so long as it does not violate the stated principles and policies of the federation to which it belongs.

In general, *craft* unions cross industry lines in that they have members in various industries, while *industrial* unions function within a particular industry, covering both craft and production workers. Some internationals logically have both craft and industrial functions. For example, the International Brotherhood of Electrical Workers operates as a craft union in construction but as an industrial union in the electrical equipment industry. The United Brotherhood of Carpenters and Joiners has craft locals in construction work and industrial locals in the wood products industry.

The distinctions between craft and industrial unions are no longer as clear as they once were, but within the AFL-CIO 15 internationals are affiliated with the Building and Construction Trades Department. These include the Asbestos Workers, the Bricklayers, the Carpenters and Joiners, the Electrical Workers, the Iron Workers, the Laborers, the Operating Engineers, the Painters, the Plasterers and Cement Masons, the Plumbers and Pipe Fitters, the Roofers, and the Sheet Metal Workers. The Industrial Union Department of the AFL-CIO has some 50 affiliates, including the Boilermakers, seven of the craft unions listed above, and virtually all of the larger predominantly industrial unions, such as the Auto Workers, Clothing and Textile Workers, the Electrical Workers, the Ladies' Garment Workers, the Machinists, the Oil and Chemical Workers, the Paperworkers, the Rubber Workers, the Steelworkers, the Transport Workers, and the Woodworkers.

As discussed in Chapter 2, the first unions were local in character, for the most part because their interests were locally defined and limited by economic forces. By the mid-nineteenth century, it was clear to increasing numbers of workers and their unions that national organization was required to cope with the employment problems of national markets and nationwide industries.

A number of present-day international unions were originally formed by numerous local unions who joined together in a single nationwide organization. Others have been formed by locals splitting off from one international union and forming another. Most of the industrial unions which date back to the 1930s were formed by organizing committees of the CIO, such as the Steelworkers Organizing Committee (SWOC), which recruited new members as well as existing company unions and dissident AFL locals.

Regardless of origin, the main responsibilities of present-day international unions—whether craft, industrial, or some combination—are to organize workers in their area(s) of jurisdiction and to provide services for their members, such as collective bargaining negotiation and contract administration.

The supreme authority and sole legislative body of the international union is its general convention, attended by voting delegates from all of its local units. Since the convention is the final authority on most union issues, the manner in which delegates are chosen and the voting power distributed is an important determinant of an international's relative degree of participatory democracy. The frequency of meeting is another significant determinant, since, as a rule, the more frequently a union meets in general convention, the greater the degree of influence and control by the membership.

In 1983, international conventions were scheduled annually by 34 percent of all unions, every three years by 9 percent, and every five years by 18 percent. One reason international unions do not hold conventions more frequently is their cost. For a large union, convention costs can run well in excess of $1 million.

In most international unions, the general officers are nominated and elected by the convention delegates. Several nominate and elect officers by referendum vote of the entire union membership; a few nominate candidates at the convention and then vote by membership referendum.

Like the AFL-CIO, whose structural aspects are taken in many cases from those of its affiliates, all international unions have an executive board or executive council whose responsibility it is to implement the decisions of the convention and to oversee the day-today policies of the union. Board membership generally includes the international president, a secretary-treasurer, and a constitutionally specified number of vice-presidents chosen on a regional or occupational basis.

By constitution, the responsibilities of the typical executive board include issuing and withdrawing local union charters, hearing administrative appeals of international union policies from locals and other subordinate bodies, passing judgment on disputed actions of international officers, selecting financial auditors, and overseeing official union publications. In practice, most international union executive boards spend much of their time dealing with collective bargaining issues and with internal problems of personnel and policy administration.

The bulk of international union resources is devoted to organizing and collective bargaining activities. The organizational structure for accomplishing these tasks varies from union to union, most often depending on the nature of the craft or industry, that is, the nature of the labor market (local, regional, or national). Some unions, such as the Steelworkers, conduct their activities almost entirely from international and regional headquarters, while others, such as the Service Employees, operate more effectively on a local basis.

At the heart of the international union's service organization are the elected or appointed staff representatives, who also sometimes function as international organizers. Typically, the staff representative assists with collective bargaining at the local level, represents the union and its members before government labor agencies, and, in general, fills requests for information and service from the members of locals he or she is assigned to serve. In sum, the staff representative is the liaison between the local and the international union; good staff representatives not only make sure that their constituents receive the best possible assistance *from* the international but also communicate the day-to-day desires and needs of the membership *to* the international.

In addition to contract negotiation and administrative services, international unions provide a variety of other valuable services to their local unions. Important among these are strike benefits (although these are typically minimal), legal services, and research and education programs which would otherwise be unavailable to all but the very largest or most wealthy local unions. Altogether, the sizable resources, financial and otherwise, available to local unions from their internationals explain in large part why less than two percent of total union membership is in individual, independent units.

The Local Union: Foundation of the Labor Movement

The policies and programs of international unions are carried out primarily at the local level. Local unions are the focal point of the collective bargaining process, as well as protecting other economic interests of the international. It is normally the local union which is responsible for administering the collective bargaining agreement, including processing members' grievances, formulating bargaining demands, and ratifying contracts. In short, although local unions exist at the pleasure of their parent organizations, international unions could not exist or function effectively without the moral, financial, and administrative support of their local units.

Most important, to the individual member the local union *is* the union in most respects. The local is the member's point of contact with other organized workers in the trade or industry; it is the agent for better wages and working conditions; and it is the source of worker-oriented educational and political programs.

Locals of industrial unions are usually organized on a plant basis, while those of craft unions generally cover a number of employers in a given geographic area. Regardless of organizational form, virtually all local unions are chartered by their parent internationals, and they are in most respects smaller facsimiles of their internationals, with a president, a secretary-treasurer, an executive board, and various committees and other officials. They have their own bylaws, in accord with the constitution of the international. The officers of local unions are elected at membership meetings rather than by convention or referendum.

Most local unions are highly political organizations. In contrast to international union officers, who tend to succeed themselves with considerable regularity, local union officers have a generally high rate of turnover. This is probably because of the greater degree of direct democratic participation at the local level compared to that of the international.

To maintain continuity and expertise, many larger local unions pay full-time business agents and assistants to manage the day-to-day business of the local. Most other local officers continue to hold their regular jobs and do their union work on a part-time, voluntary basis. The functions of the business agent typically include such local union activities as maintaining office files, arranging meeting agendas, and participating in the negotiation and administration of collective bargaining agreements along with other local officers and/or international representatives. Additionally, in the building and construction trades, business agents are in charge of local hiring halls, which gives them considerable power and influence over employment opportunities for the members.

The smaller locals of industrial unions have traditionally relied on unpaid officers and executive board members to handle union affairs and to represent members both on and off the job. In larger locals, however—with or without a business agent—it is not unusual to find at least one full-time officer paid by the local union.

The local union meeting is the vehicle by which the membership determines the policies and activities of the union. The business of the local union meeting generally includes discussion of work- and contract-related problems as well as financial and other routine administrative considerations.

An important function of the local union is enforcing the international's standards of conduct for its members. Members who violate international or local rules may be disciplined by reprimand, fine, suspension, or, in the most severe cases, expulsion from the union. Union rules of conduct commonly cover such infractions as providing false information about the union or its officers, misappropriating union funds, refusing to picket, and strikebreaking. Additionally, a number of union constitutions prohibit membership in any group or organization which espouses totalitarian principles.

Abuse of internal union disciplinary procedures has never been widespread in unions as a whole. However, the occasional flagrant disregard of members' rights by some unions prompted the Landrum-Griffin legislation in 1959 specifying that no union member can be disciplined, fined, or expelled without first receiving the charges in writing, being given a reasonable time to prepare a defense, and accorded a full and fair hearing. Subsequent to Landrum-Griffin, a number of international unions strengthened and clarified their constitutions to further protect the rights of individual members. Today, according to most observers, internal union discipline is handled almost exclusively within the law.

Local Union Service Activities

Quite apart from their job-related collective bargaining functions, many local unions are involved in a wide range of community service activities, such as support of the United Way and other charitable institutions. Thousands of union members volunteer time to youth, drug and alcohol abuse counseling, and similar local programs which benefit the community as a whole.

Although labor is still relatively underrepresented in most community activities, the number of union representatives on the advisory boards of community and charitable organizations has been steadily increasing. This increase reflects a growing acceptance of unions as a legitimate element of community life and as a valuable resource in these service activities.

Institutional Constraints and Considerations

From the foregoing, it is obvious that unions are basically service organizations. In theory at least, they have no reason to exist other than for the benefit of their members. From the local union to the international and federation levels, the structure of the American labor movement is designed to meet the needs of workers, to protect and enhance their economic, social, and political interests both on and off the job. But the realities of the American economy are such that numerous factors have frustrated the practical attainment of union goals and objectives, especially in terms of advancing the interests of members on the job.

Problems of Finance and Administration

To meet the needs of their members in a complex and rapidly changing economy, unions have developed increasingly sophisticated collective bargaining concepts and processes over the years. Examples of this trend include multifirm and multiplant contracts; pension, insurance, and supplemental unemployment benefits; and cost-of-living and relocation allowances. But these advances have carried high price tags. International unions have incurred increasing costs in form of salaries for technical personnel (lawyers, industrial engineers, accountants, economists, insurance and pension experts, etc.) and equipment (namely, computers and other technical hardware), and the funds for these needed items can come from only one place—the membership.

In 1955, the typical union member paid dues of around $3 per month. By 1985, the figure was close to $15. This fivefold increase is largely explained, of course, by inflation (300 percent over the period), but it also reflects the greater *absolute* level of funding required to service the union member today compared to 30 years ago. As a way of sharing the costs of representation more equitably, a current trend is for union members to pay dues equal to two hours per month or about one percent of their regular wages.

Additionally, the labor movement has paid a price in that increasing financial requirements have meant that many smaller unions must face the dilemma of raising their dues to what the members would consider intolerably high levels, cutting back on services, or going out of existence (usually by merging with another union). The last of these three alternatives has been particularly noticeable in recent years. In 1955, at the time of the merger, there were 142 unions affiliated with the AFL-CIO (110 AFL and 32 CIO). By 1985, the number had fallen to 96. But while the number of affiliates fell by a third, total membership increased by 25 percent, resulting in a much larger average membership per union. This trend toward larger international unions reflects economic realities; many unions simply cannot operate efficiently with a small membership base.

The vast majority of unions which disappeared in the last 20 years did not do so literally; they merged out of economic necessity with other smaller unions or with a larger international able to offer the services they could no longer finance on their own. The recent merger of the Aluminum, Brick and Clay, and Glass and Ceramic Workers into a 47,000-member international is an example of smaller union combinations, that of the Jewelry Workers with the Service Employees an example of a small international joining a much larger one.

In the early 1980s, merger talks were in progress among at least 20 different international unions, most of them prompted by increased operating expenses. There is every reason to believe this trend will continue; as of 1983, there were still 40 international unions in the United States with fewer than 10,000 members.[6] The problem, however, is not limited to the smallest unions. Recently many larger unions also have experienced extreme financial hardship, most often from the double squeeze of rising costs and falling membership.

Critics of the labor movement, however, give little consideration to the financial woes of international unions. Instead, they often call attention to what they see as proof of labor "bossism" and

[6]In 1984, 57 of 95 unions affiliated with the AFL-CIO had fewer than 100,000 members.

financial irresponsibility in the salaries received by some top labor officials. They cite, for example, the $400,000 plus salary received by the president of the International Brotherhood of Teamsters in 1985. But high salaries are by far the exception among international union presidents and other top labor officials. The overwhelming majority of international union presidents' salaries are currently in the $50,000-$75,000 range, which is well in line with the salaries of other executives in the country.

The compensation problem in unions overall is not one of excess but rather of keeping salaries high enough to be able to compete in the marketplace with other employers for staff and other professional employees. Many unions are simply unable to offer the benefits available in other areas of employment. As a whole, and without discounting the occasional abuses that do exist, it can be said fairly that dedication far outweighs financial excess as a characteristic of officials in the American labor movement.

Union Democracy and Leadership Development

A speaker at a 1978 national meeting of union and university labor educators made a startling comment about unions and the labor movement today compared with 40 years ago. In the 1940s, he said, both workers and their leaders, especially at the international union level, had very similar views on the policies and procedures necessary in the labor movement. The economic and political security of both groups was highly uncertain, and what benefited the membership necessarily benefited the union as well. What was good for the rank and file was also good for the leadership.

But today, the speaker asserted, at least what the rank and file perceives as its needs (greater local union automony, for example) is often quite different from what the leadership perceives as its needs (in the case of the example above, more centralized control over the complexities of collective bargaining and contract administration). The 1973 agreement between the steel industry and the United Steelworkers of America, which removed the strike from the union's arsenal of master contract bargaining weapons, is an excellent example of such differences. Even though the workers received considerable economic benefits in return for the union's promise not to strike over the terms of the basic steel agreement, many individuals within the union felt that the potential losses from giving up their strongest bargaining tool far outweighed immediate or even future gains.

On one hand, it is in the best interests of unions (international *and* local) as well as employers to avoid costly strikes; on the other hand, many feel that without numerous strikes or at least their threat over the years, neither the unions nor their members would have achieved the gains they have. In some respects, the controversy appears to boil down to whether the union as an institution exists for the benefit of the membership or whether the membership exists for the benefit of the union.

The long-range success of international unions depends on the extent to which they meet the needs of their members. Increasingly, however, different institutional settings, including the greater financial and political security of some international unions and their officers relative to local unions and their members, have caused the operational philosophies of the two groups to diverge. Thus, while decreasing militancy may be called for at the international union level, just the opposite may be sought at the local level. For example, the diplomatic tactics required of international union officers to settle complex contract issues in a multiemployer contract are understandably quite different from those used by the local business agent in resolving day-to-day problems at the job site.

The problems of diverging operational philosophies have been compounded by the growing size and complexity of union organizations. To maintain continuity of leadership and high levels of technical expertise, international unions have tended to become more centralized and bureaucratic by both circumstance and design. In fact, the efforts of some unions to remain open and responsive to the needs and desires of the membership have perhaps been detrimental to their success at the bargaining table, leading to the ironic judgment by some observers that a few unions are too democratic for their own good.

Obviously, the answer to the question of who will run the union—the members or the officers—lies somewhere between the extremes of complete centralization and complete local autonomy. And the answer to whether the union exists for the benefit of the members or vice versa is "neither." The international union, of course, could not exist without members, but in the complex economic and political environment of industrial America, neither could individual workers or local groups of workers advance their job interests without the support of some centralized organization with resources more equal to those of the employers. Indeed, this mutual interdependence explains much of the structure and functions of the labor movement as we know them today. A federated labor movement composed of international unions and their chartered local unions is logical. The difficulty lies in ensuring that the various parts complement, rather than compete with, each other.

In large part, the solution to the dilemma of centralization versus local autonomy in the labor movement can be found in utilizing both philosophies, that is, by enhancing the effective militance of the local union as well as professional maturity at the international and federation levels, and making them work together. This can be accomplished via democratic procedures to increase membership participation for the purpose of developing effective leadership at all levels. Unfortunately, in a few international unions, such a gulf has developed between the membership and the leadership that the reestablishment of mutual trust and cooperation may present enormous challenges.

Issues of Education and Communication

Recently, increasing efforts have been made to resolve conflicts between the leadership and the membership of many unions, both craft and industrial. Most notable has been the establishment of numerous rank-and-file movements to press for democratic reforms, both in specific unions and in the labor movement at large. At the same time, and often in response to rank-and-file pressures, the leadership of some international unions has initiated its own programs to deal with these problems. In some cases, the efforts of the membership and the leadership have been complementary, leading to significant improvements; in others, competition and bitterness have resulted in deteriorating trust and a lack of cooperation by both groups.

It is important to remember that internal conflict is nothing new to the American labor movement; in fact, both theoretical and practical differences account for the very origins of many of the unions in this country. What is different today compared to 40 to 50 years ago is that present conflicts are more *within* than *between* unions. The differences within unions today fall into two broad categories. One category includes very practical considerations of how best to conduct union affairs given the diversity of our society and the traditional role of unions therein. The other category involves more theoretical questions which challenge the past and present philosophy of the American labor movement, namely, its acceptance of capitalism and its decision to work within the system rather than trying to replace it.

This distinction between practical and theoretical differences is important. It is complicated by the fact that practical and theoretical disagreements may often become intertwined, leading to confusion over the issues at stake as well as the motives of the antagonists.

For example, the rank-and-file movements within many international unions began quite simply on the basis of very practical disagreements over internal union policies such as procedures for the election of local officers, membership ratification of contracts, and the control of union pension funds. But such practical challenges were often considered by the union leadership to be theoretical attacks. A considerable element of revolutionary unionism was interpretatively imposed on these conflicts, sometimes leading individuals to perceive philosophical differences where none really existed.

There is nothing wrong with theoretical debate over goals and objectives of the union. In fact, numerous observers have pointed to the absence of such debate within the larger American labor movement as a cause of its relative lack of growth and social vigor in recent years. Within the labor movement, it is desirable to encourage debate over goals and objectives as well as procedures. But at the same time, the parties should clearly understand the institutional framework within which they discuss their differences.

Rank-and-file advocates should remember that their international union officers are often restrained by the legal, political, and economic systems within which they function and that logical short-range solutions may sometimes have disastrous long-range effects. Likewise, union officers need to understand that to many individual members, there *is* no long run; it is only the present that counts. Officers must also accept the fact that the needs of the membership are indeed often different from those of the organization as an entity itself.

To distinguish theoretical and philosophical differences from those of practice and procedure, for example, better education programs and communication between and among the various levels of the labor movement can reduce misunderstanding and can bond the rank and file and the leadership into a united front.

In the final analysis, unions must function as effectively as possible within the present context of institutional restraints and considerations. At the same time, if unions are to regain their social and economic momentum, their members and leaders must search for new goals as well as procedures to further advance the labor movement.

Unions in the Political Arena

An excellent example of union activity in full recognition of its institutional place in society can be seen in labor's involvement in politics. The nature of political activity by unions today did not develop by accident. It grew out of the experience and needs of unions as they assumed a particularly structured, well-defined, and legally limited role in the economic affairs of American industrial society.

As we have already learned from our review of American labor history, union involvement in politics is not a recent phenomenon. As far back as 1828, organized workers in Philadelphia ran their own candidates for public office. In 1834 and 1836, Ely Moore, president of the National Trades Union, was elected to Congress from the state of New York. In the 1860s and 1870s, the National Labor Union strongly urged union participation in politics (in 1872, the NLU even nominated its own candidates for President and Vice President), and later the Knights of Labor supported hundreds and elected scores of their own candidates.

Under Samuel Gompers (whose unsuccessful bid for election to the New York state constitutional convention in 1893 may have influenced his philosophy), the AFL developed a firm policy of no direct involvement in politics. In contrast to its predecessors, the AFL chose to concentrate on indirect participation, as embodied in its 1906 convention declaration of "rewarding labor's friends and defeating its enemies." Although there is still considerable debate among labor economists and historians over the long-range effects of this decision on the labor movement, the survival of the AFL confirmed the wisdom of a pragmatic philosophy for that time.

In large part, Gompers and the AFL rejected direct political action by labor because they perceived American workers as being different from their European counterparts. The political affiliation of American workers, they reasoned, was determined by inheritance, religion, geography, and many other forces, in contrast to European society, where workers were thrown into a natural working-class-conscious political alliance as a matter of birth. Thus, to Gompers and the AFL, earlier attempts to form a federation of trade unionists had failed because the European *class-conscious* variety of trade unionism could not be successfully adapted to *job-conscious* American workers. What the American labor movement needed was *business unionism,* where job interests took precedence over class and political interests.

But AFL political policy began to change in the early 1900s

with the recognition that the labor movement, even while promoting principles of business unionism, required favorable state and federal legislation if it was to succeed. Thus the AFL became more active in politics through its efforts to see that sympathetic officials were named to important labor positions in government and that organized labor was adequately represented on tripartite government panels (labor, management, and the public).

The Great Depression and the Roosevelt era increased labor's political involvement for three reasons in particular. First, the growth of organized labor from some three million members to more than 14 million in just 12 years (1932–1944) increasingly meant that labor had to be considered a political force. Fourteen million union members, together with friends and families, were too powerful a bloc of voters to be ignored.

Second, the Great Depression changed the view of organized labor, especially the AFL, toward the role of government. Prior to the 1930s, labor in general had been suspicious of government, and for good reason, since the powers of government had usually been exercised in favor of management. But the total failure of the private economy to provide social and economic security for workers during the Depression, in conjunction with the New Deal's increasing emphasis on human rights relative to property rights, convinced the labor movement that it too could get a new and better "deal" from government. Finally, the advent of the CIO contributed to a broader political outlook within the labor movement. As a whole, the CIO was politically more progressive than the AFL; the very struggle for industrial unionism had been a radicalizing experience for its proponents.

Thus by the time the two labor federations, the AFL and the CIO, merged in 1955, they actually represented a new form of unionism, described by labor economist Joseph Shister at the time as "social unionism."

The numerical strength of the labor movement, combined with its acceptance of capitalism and a legitimate role for government in labor-management relations, made it both logical and necessary for labor to increase its political involvement. It is important to note that it did so not only in regard to job problems of the organized but also with respect to broader social and economic matters of concern to all workers, organized or not.

The passage of the Taft-Hartley Act in 1947 shocked the labor movement; after struggling for 150 years to achieve collective bar-

Plant closing demonstration in Oshawa, Ontario, Canada, 1981.

UAW Solidarity Magazine/Cochran

gaining rights gained under the Wagner Act, labor had lost considerable power to employers after only 12 years.

Following the Taft-Hartley setback, the AFL organized Labor's League for Political Education (LLPE) and, along with the CIO Political Action Committee (PAC) which had been founded in 1943, began extensive programs to educate union members on labor issues and to support labor candidates (Republican or Democratic) through campaigns to register and get out the vote on Election Day.

Subsequent to the AFL-CIO merger, the Committee on Political Education (COPE) was formed, combining LLPE and PAC activities. Today, thousands of AFL-CIO union members serve as volunteers on area central body COPE committees that endorse local political candidates via extensive interviews on their positions regarding issues of importance to labor. COPE committees also conduct registration and voter turnout campaigns. At the state and national levels, candidates for national office are endorsed by state federations.

In addition to endorsement and election activities, COPE and its counterparts in most independent unions raise contributions from individual union members for financial support of endorsed candidates (the Taft-Hartley Act outlawed the use of union funds for political purposes in connection with any federal election).

As of 1978, over 20 international unions, including the Machinists, Operating Engineers, Teachers, and Sheet Metal Workers, had begun payroll deduction programs for voluntary contributions to political funds; many others, including the Boilermakers, Clothing and Textile Workers, and the United Association (plumbers and pipefitters), were considering them. In spite of these and other new efforts to raise labor "campaign funds," however, corporate political contributions remained many times greater than those of workers.

Another important aspect of labor's current political activity is legislative lobbying, primarily at the state and national levels, by unions and their federations. At the state level, the AFL-CIO, often in alliance with independent unions such as the United Mine Workers and the Teamsters, works for the introduction and passage of enabling and protective legislation supportive of workers and their families. State labor lobbyists, for example, are especially active in the areas of workers' and unemployment compensation programs, since these benefits are legislated at the state level.

At the national level, unions and their federations lobby over an extremely wide range of legislation. As a partial indication of this

Key Words and Phrases

- AFL-CIO Committee on Political Education (COPE)
- AFL-CIO Department of Organization and Field Services
- AFL-CIO departments
- AFL-CIO Executive Council
- AFL-CIO General Board
- AFL-CIO local central body
- AFL-CIO standing committees
- AFL-CIO state central body
- Assembly of Government Employees
- centralization
- class consciousness
- continuity of leadership
- democratic reforms
- economic sector
- employee association
- federal labor union (AFL)
- federated labor movement
- human rights versus property rights
- International Confederation of Free Trade Unions
- International Labor Organization
- international organizer
- international trade secretariat
- international union staff representative
- jurisdictional disputes
- Labor's League for Political Education
- legislative lobbying
- local industrial union (CIO)
- local union
- local union autonomy
- local union business agent
- multiplant and multi-employer bargaining
- National Federation of Independent Unions
- national union
- participatory democracy
- per capita payments
- Political Action Committee
- Railway Labor Executives Association
- social unionism
- Steelworkers Organizing Committee (SWOC)
- strike benefits
- union mergers
- unions as service organizations
- voluntary federation

fact, the 1985 AFL-CIO convention passed resolutions on nearly 100 different legislative issues, and there are literally hundreds of other day-to-day, less significant issues on which organized labor expresses its opinion to Congress and the White House.

Today American unions still rely primarily on collective bargaining with employers to achieve their economic goals. But simultaneously there is the awareness that unless unions remain active in politics, what is won at the bargaining table may be legislated away by government. And in the case of legislation, without continuing vigilance by labor what has been gained through law may also be lost through law.

Review and Discussion Questions

1. Describe the organization and composition of the American labor movement with particular reference to its demographics and its relative strength in various geographic areas and economic sectors.
2. In what ways have the forces of history, technology, and law helped to shape the structure and functions of the American labor movement?
3. The AFL-CIO is a "federation." What does this mean? Describe the structure and functions of the AFL-CIO.
4. What are the functions of local and state labor federations?
5. Does the fact that certain large international unions are not affiliated with the AFL-CIO affect its power and influence? Explain.
6. What are the main reasons that the American labor movement is involved in international affairs?
7. Describe the structure and functions of the international union and its place in the labor movement as a whole.
8. What are the meaning and justification for this chapter's reference to local unions as the *foundation* of the labor movement?
9. What factors have contributed to the upward movement of power and influence (i.e., centralization) in the American labor movement? Is greater decentralization likely or possible, or even desirable?
10. Explain the most significant reasons for the recent increased merger activity among international unions.
11. What is meant by the statement that some unions are too democratic for their own good? To what extent does union democracy conflict with union effectiveness?
12. What do you think is the greatest weakness in union government? What changes would you suggest to correct this weakness?
13. Explain the increasing involvement of labor in politics. Why is it that so many rank-and-file unionists are opposed to their union's political activities? What might be done to counter these objections?

Chapter Resources and Suggested Further Reading

Complete bibliographical information for the following titles can be found in the Bibliography.

Bloom and Northrup, *Economics of Labor Relations.*

Clifford, *Directory of U.S. Labor Organizations.*

Cohen, "Institutional Aspects of Unionism," in *Labor in the United States.*

Estey, "Anatomy of the Labor Movement" and "The Management of Unions," in *The Unions: Structure, Development, and Management.*

Marshall, Briggs, and King, *Labor Economics.*
Shister, *Economics of the Labor Market.*
Wallihan, *Union Government and Organization in the United States.*

Take not from the mouth of labor the bread it has earned.
—Thomas Jefferson, Inaugural Address, 1801

Peace will never be entirely secure until men everywhere have learned to conquer poverty without sacrificing liberty or security.
—Norman Thomas, circa 1940

Civilization must be judged and prized, not by the amount of power it has developed, but how much it has evolved and given expression, by its laws and institutions, to the love of humanity.
—Rabindranath Tagore, 1914

Every new opinion, at its starting, is precisely in a minority of one.
—Thomas Carlyle, 1840

5

Collective Bargaining: Contract Negotiations*

. . . to bargain collectively is the performance of the mutual obligation of the employer and the representative of the employees to meet at reasonable times and confer in good faith with respect to wages, hours, and other terms and conditions of employment, on the negotiation of an agreement, or any question arising thereunder. . . .

—Section 8 (d), National Labor Relations Act (1935)

SETTING THE FRAMEWORK

The preceding four chapters have described the *form* of the American labor movement. The remaining chapters deal more specifically with the *content* of labor relations, beginning with contract negotiations and concluding with a discussion of contemporary problems and trends. As a background for studying these subjects in detail, it will be helpful to review the important historical and legal developments that have shaped the form as well as the content of labor relations in the United States.

The development of collective bargaining can be viewed chronologically, that is, as a series of contrasting historical periods involving different legal and other institutional relationships between workers and their employers. Another way of looking at this progression is to consider the institution of collective bargaining itself as part of a larger system of economic and social relationships for society as a whole. Actually, these two approaches are complemen-

*This chapter is based largely on the writings of Beal, Wickersham, and Kienast; Lester; and Richardson. See Chapter Resources and Bibliography for specific references.

tary; thus, we will consider them together as a way to establish a framework for analyzing the collective bargaining process in detail.

Chronology of Collective Bargaining Development

The evolution of collective bargaining in America can be divided roughly into two general periods of approximately 100 years each: the first from the post-revolutionary period until roughly 1890; the second, which in turn can be divided into four subperiods of varying length, from 1890 to the present.

It is important to remember that during the years prior to the emergence of an industrial economy in the late nineteenth century, workers, their unions, and employers did not engage in the give-and-take of collective bargaining as we know and understand it today. This period was marked by "unilateralism" in labor relations. When conditions (usually economic ones) were favorable, workers were sometimes able to extract concessions from their employers on a "take it or leave it" basis. Employers were likewise unilateral in their actions—either ignoring the demands of workers or acceding until a time when previous union gains could be unilaterally abolished.

The economic, social, and political environment within which unilateralism was the most evident characteristic of labor relations for more than a century must be understood as a truly evolutionary period in American industrial history. Basic economic changes in products and markets effected new forms of ownership and production and, as a result, brought about fundamental changes in the nature of work and in relations between workers and their employers. For the emerging labor movement, these changes meant organizational and operational experimentation until unions finally evolved by the 1880s to a structure and philosophy basically compatible with other American economic institutions. Whether by accident or design, the AFL's business unionism presented employers with a minimally acceptable process for at least dealing with the demands of skilled workers.

During the four-plus decades from the establishment of the AFL to the beginning of the Great Depression, collective bargaining in the form of bilaterally established "trade agreements" became increasingly prevalent. Beginning with the "stove molders agreement of 1891" and continuing in other industries such as clothing, coal mining, the railroads, and building construction, the sustained coexistence of organized labor and organized capital—even on adversary terms—signaled growing acceptance of union legitimacy and the concept of collective bargaining. As evidence of this change, the Federal Government adopted a selectively neutral stance toward unions and collective bargaining, moving from open hostility during the Pullman strike in 1894 to official encouragement with the passage of the Railway Labor Act in 1926.

The period from the beginning of the Great Depression through the end of World War II brought together social, economic, and political forces which had been operating for the preceding four decades. Prompted by the crisis of western capitalism, the Federal Government made numerous concessions to save the system from total collapse. For workers and unions, the passage of the Norris-LaGuardia Act, the National Industrial Recovery Act and, finally, the National Labor Relations Act brought to collective bargaining an acceptance and respectability previously unobtainable through efforts in the private sector alone. By protecting workers' freedom of association and "encouraging the practice and procedure of collective bargaining," federal law established a framework for the next stage of development in labor relations: employer acceptance.

By the end of World War II, more than 100,000 collective bargaining agreements were in effect, covering a total of some 15 million workers and virtually every major industry in the country. Although the strike activity of the immediate postwar period served as a rationale for restricting the rights of labor established by the Wagner Act, neither the Taft-Hartley Act in 1947 nor the Landrum-Griffin Act of 1959 sought to abolish collective bargaining. Rather, they redefined the rules for the process and attempted to mold the various components of labor relations into forms less disruptive to the other major institutions of society. No longer at issue was the right of unions to exist or to negotiate collective bargaining agreements for their members. Instead, by the late 1950s and early 1960s, attention focused on whether the collective bargaining process could continue to function effectively in the face of new national and international problems on a variety of economic, social, and political fronts.

There was no sharp transition from post-World War II to contemporary labor relations, but the two periods can be clearly contrasted in at least two important respects. First, after experiencing several years of absolute decline because of failure to adjust to industrial and occupational shifts in employment, the labor movement began a period of new growth in the early 1960s—largely as a result of the extension of union organizing and collective bargaining to public employees at the local, state, and federal levels. Second, and related to their growth among white collar workers, unions demonstrated their ability to deal with the more complex issues of the 1960s and 1970s.

Still, the continued effects of antiunion legislation and anticommunist hysteria in the 1940s and 1950s, and the growing economic instabilities of the 1960s and 1970s served to weaken the postwar labor movement over time. At present, many observers doubt that American unions in their present form will be able to deal adequately with the heightening crises of capital flight, unstable energy supplies, foreign competition, and union busting facing their members in the 1980s. But despite the current wave of employer opposition, collective bargaining itself is now recognized as a firmly established and viable institution with the potential for making significant contributions in resolving the problems of workers and other organized groups in society.

Collective Bargaining as Part of the Larger Social System

John T. Dunlop, in his 1958 book *Industrial Relations Systems*, theorized that collective bargaining is part of a larger labor relations system which in turn is part of the general social system. The labor relations system, he said, can be studied in terms of three institutional contexts: the market context; the context of technology at the workplace; and the context of various power and influence relationships in the larger society, as reflected in the workplace. Thus, according to Dunlop, the form and content of collective bargaining in a particular sector of economic activity or at a given workplace are largely determined by and thus explainable within these three basic frameworks.

The Market Context

Under capitalism, the provision of goods and services—whether in the private (business) or public (government) sector—is largely dependent upon demand in the marketplace. As a result, all enterprises are limited, especially in the long run, by what their products/services will sell for on the market. This phenomenon is most obvious in the private sector of the economy, where what people want has an effect on the goods and services offered for sale. For example, beginning in the late 1970s, the increase in consumer demand for more energy-efficient automobiles (a result of price increases in another marketplace—that of gasoline) prompted manufacturers to offer cars with higher gas-mileage ratings. But the market context affects the public sector as well. "Sunset laws," which require government agencies to show periodically that the demand for their goods and/or services still exists and is indeed being met, are a good example of how the market can influence public sector activity.

Technology at the Workplace

The demand for goods and services in the marketplace has a direct effect on how those goods and services will be produced. Most important to the study of collective bargaining, the kinds of jobs that are created and their relation to each other are basically functions of technology at the workplace. The complexities of the context of technology at the workplace can be illustrated by using the housing industry as an example of the three fundamental technologies involved.

Most higher priced residential construction involves *handicraft* technology, where raw materials (lumber, concrete, glass, etc.) are transformed into a finished product (a house) by skilled craft workers, working with their hands and with hand tools. The market for this residential housing is such that, with specific differences from unit to unit, each house produced by these craft workers is unique. But even though an identical house may never before have been constructed, no one has to tell the skilled construction worker *how* to do the job—only *what* needs to be done.

Another segment of the housing market includes prefabricated and mobile homes; this type of construction involves *mass production* technology. In contrast to handicraft technology, mass production involves standardized units which are assembled by semiskilled or unskilled workers using their hands or hand tools and machines; some assistance may be provided by a few skilled workers. Each worker is trained to do only one of numerous specific tasks involved in producing the final product. Thus, the mass production worker is told not only what needs to be done but also how to do it.

The third workplace technology is that of automation, where the products (such as nails, electrical wire, and mortar) are produced entirely by machines, without any direct human effort. Skilled craft workers maintain the machines; semiskilled workers operate the machines; and unskilled workers may physically supply the machines with raw materials.

Historically, changes in markets and workplace technology have helped shape the nature and content of work as we know it today. In general, the widespread use of handicraft technology has been replaced by mass production, which in turn has increasingly given way to automation. It seems inevitable, however, that some combination of all three technologies will continue in order to meet different consumer and producer needs.

The Context of Power and Influence Relationships

Industrial relations and therefore collective bargaining is basically an economic relationship between workers and owners/managers. But there is also a significant element of social and political content to the process. Simply stated, the social, political, and economic position of workers and managers outside the workplace has an effect on their relationships inside the workplace. For example, the lower social status of unskilled factory workers relative to skilled craft workers, in addition to the fact that they were more easily replaced, was a longtime barrier to their union organization; today, migrant farm workers are disadvantaged by their relative powerlessness in legislative circles. The owners and managers of business enterprises are affected, not only by the relative status and power of their employees, but also by their own positions of power and influence in the larger community. Thus, the nature and content of labor relations at any given workplace will depend on the combined economic, social, and political environments of both workers and managers.

Government, which is basically responsible for establishing and administering the laws of society, is also influenced by the combined contexts of market, workplace technology, and power/influence relationships. Therefore, it is logical to assume that for society as a whole, the legal framework of labor relations will be determined by the relative impact of all of these factors.

Accordingly, the variations in labor relations systems from society to society, discussed in Chapter 7, are largely a consequence of differences in context and resultant legal frameworks.

The Participants in the Collective Bargaining Process

There are three primary groups of participants in the collective bargaining process:

(1) *Workers* and their representative organizations;

(2) *Owners/managers* and their representative associations; and

(3) *Agents* of government and other individuals who have specific roles in the collective bargaining process or who are on occasion called in by the two primary participants.

The logic of Dunlop's three labor relations contexts is apparent when considering the different forms of collective bargaining relationships that exist simultaneously in various sectors of our economy.[1] In principle, there are two basic models of industry/union organization for collective bargaining—craft and industrial. In practice, a third model can be clearly identified in some economic sectors—an "amalgamated" structure, involving both craft and industrial organization. But regardless of the model of organization, American collective bargaining always involves these three principal groups: workers, owners/managers, and third-party agents.

At present, it will be sufficient to remember that regardless of their particular form of organization, business enterprises in our society are established, continued, or disbanded almost solely on the basis of their profitability. The owners/managers of businesses seek markets, choose appropriate technologies, and hire and direct a work force because they hope to make a profit from their undertakings. Therefore, since labor is often the largest single item purchased by business, it is logical to assume that employers are motivated to hire workers at the lowest possible cost. To pay more than is absolutely necessary for a work force means less profit for the owners/managers of any business enterprise.

Therefore, although owners/managers, third-party agents, and workers may assume specific and important roles in the collective bargaining process, emphasis can be placed on workers and their organizations to explain the various models of organization. The role of third-party agents in the collective bargaining process will be discussed later.

[1]John T. Dunlop and Neil W. Chamberlain, Frontiers of Collective Bargaining (1967).

The Craft Model

In the contexts of market, workplace technology, and power and influence relationships, the construction industry is the most prominent example of the craft model of organization for collective bargaining. For the most part, the market for construction industry products is local and specialized, prompting and justifying the extensive use of handicraft technology. The craft model is typified by skilled labor as a *direct* factor of production. Without skilled craft workers, the construction contractor could not stay in business, for without these skills there could be no production. In addition, because of the length of time required to master a given craft and the relatively short time required to complete a given construction project, it is impossible for a contractor to use "on-the-job" training as a means of acquiring a work force. The employer must be able to rely on a pool of trained skilled workers, all of whom are theoretically equally qualified in a particular craft.

The nature of the market and the workplace technology thus have an effect upon power and influence relationships in the craft model. This is especially evident in the case of the workers and their representative organizations. Although the status and prestige of craft workers have apparently declined somewhat in recent years relative to other classifications of work, the independence and satisfaction of what is basically "creative" work have remained an attractive tradition to those who practice a skilled trade. Craft workers have long been aware of their relatively higher status in the labor force and thus in the larger social community. They also have been aware that maintaining that status, both economically and socially, depends on successfully resisting changes that could erode their position. Thus, the unions of craft workers have been traditionally conservative in their organizational goals and operational objectives. Given the very real threats of mass production and automation technologies and their accompanying pressure to expand production beyond the local market, craft unions are understandably inclined to resist technological and other innovations in their jurisdiction. Skilled workers are a *direct* factor of production in the craft model of labor relations organization; any fundamental change, especially in the context of markets or workplace technology, can, therefore, be expected to have a direct effect on the status and welfare of craft unions and the workers they represent.

The Industrial Model

In contrast to the basically local market and handicraft technology associated with the craft model of labor relations organization, the industrial model is generally typified by mass production technology (the assembly line) and mass consumption markets (national and international).

Mass production technology is based on the *division of labor,* that is, the breaking down of production processes that formerly required skilled craft workers into a series of component tasks that can be performed by properly trained, unskilled (although expert) operators using machines and hand tools.

The long list of products in use today that were once produced by skilled craft workers provides evidence of the pervasive effects of mass production and automation technologies on the nature and content of work. For example, as late as the early twentieth century, the nation's iron and steel mills were operated largely by skilled craft workers whose union, the Amalgamated Association of Iron and Steel Workers, AFL, we referred to in Chapter 2. Today, the steel industry is a mass production industry, structured much like the auto industry, the garment industry, and many others that have done away with handicraft technology in the pursuit of expanded markets and greater profits. Steelworkers today are almost exclusively members of industrial unions, in particular the United Steelworkers of America, which was originally a CIO affiliate.

The difference between skill and expertise is important in comparing the workplace technology of the craft and industrial models of labor relations organization. Skill may be defined as being associated with apprenticeship (whether formal or informal)—that is, mastering the range of theoretical knowledge and practical work procedures of one of the recognized crafts. By contrast, mass production workers, although they are often referred to as skilled, are more correctly viewed as specialists in one particular aspect of work. Through aptitude, in conjunction with training and experience, they are able to develop a high level of expertise.

For example, some forklift operators are extremely adept at maneuvering their equipment in tight spaces, while others lack the combination of aptitude, training, and experience necessary to accomplish such feats. In fact, some forklift operators have developed a higher degree of expertise than others. But in terms of skill, it is the vehicle mechanic whose theoretical and practical knowledge is called into play when the forklift breaks down and is in need of repair.

The distinction between skill and expertise derives from the organization of work itself—craft compared to industrial. Handicraft production is necessarily organized around the individual craft *worker* as a direct factor of production. But mass production emphasizes the production *unit* (usually a factory) as a whole; individual workers are separate and "replaceable parts" of an integrated system.

As for power and influence relationships, the social and economic position of mass production workers historically has been lower than that of craft workers, in part because they lacked the skill and independence of craft workers and thus were more easily prevented from organizing and exercising their potential power in the marketplace. But over a period of time two factors have tended to narrow these differences between craft and industrial workers. First, the conversion of industrial production from handicraft to mass production technologies prompted the formation of industrial unions that finally succeeded in organizing workers along factory or industry lines, rather than by skill or craft. The establishment of industrial unions whose membership includes all workers in a particular factory or industry regardless of the particular kind of work performed has given mass production workers an organizational status similar to that previously enjoyed only by skilled craft workers. Second, the high productivity of many mass production workers has justified the negotiation of high wages; as a result, the economic position of some factory workers now exceeds that of some craft workers.

Until recently, industrial unions were less concerned with changes in workplace technology than were craft unions. Industrial unions typically sought to secure the benefits of new technology for their members through negotiated forms of job security and retraining for the new jobs created by technological change. But the advent of automation has brought many of the same problems for industrial unions that craft unions faced with the introduction of mass production technology. Craft unions have traditionally resisted changes that would eliminate the need for their skills, and thus their jobs. Industrial unions are now confronted with an analogous situation. Automation has greatly reduced the need for mass production workers, whose expertise is needed less and less in the production process.

The Amalgamated Model

The amalgamated model of labor relations organization is not widespread, but it is distinctive where it is found. The garment industry is a good example of this model in operation. As the industry evolved, especially in the production of men's clothing, there was no sharp or complete transition from handicraft to mass production technologies. A long period of subcontracting resulted in many small shops which specialized in a particular stage of the garment manufacturing process. The first unions in the industry were organized among these smaller shops and were craft oriented according to the particular skill involved.

As large-scale manufacturing appeared, some companies physically reassembled the complete array of tailoring skills under one roof, and as they did so, the various component craft unions found it necessary to join together and deal with the factory as an industrial union. Both the International Ladies' Garment Workers' Union and the Amalgamated Clothing Workers Union established "joint boards" with representatives of all of the tailoring crafts, to deal not only with the large integrated manufacturers but also with the remaining specialized subcontractors.

The amalgamated labor relations model is therefore a combination of craft and industrial organization, depending on the nature of the industry—its market and workplace technology contexts. It also reflects a combination of craft- and industry-oriented power and influence relationships.

Public Employees

Special note can be made of how public employee unions conform to basic labor relations models according to the influence of the three determining contexts. The context of workplace technology is virtually the same regardless of whether employment is in the private or the public sector. For example, a diesel mechanic working for a municipal bus line has the same skills and uses the same tools as a diesel mechanic employed by Greyhound or Trailways. But the contexts of market and power/influence relationships are typically distinct.

The economic limitations imposed by the market in the private sector are paralleled by budgetary limitations in the public sector. The "market" for public employment therefore depends as much or more on political as on economic considerations. Workers in the public sector have had to rely on sympathetic politicians and favorable legislation to a much greater degree than workers in the private sector; as a result, public sector unions have had to concentrate on lobbying to realize many of the same gains achieved through collective bargaining in the private sector.

The related context of power and influence relationships has been especially critical to the form and content of labor relations in the public sector, primarily because the sovereign power of government represents an ultimate authority beyond which there is no appeal. For many years, this sovereignty has been used as a rationale for prohibiting collective bargaining in the public sector. However, the increasing militancy of public employees and their demands for bargaining rights similar to those achieved by workers in the private sector have forced government to make significant concessions.

Despite government concessions in the sovereignty area, public employee unions must still deal with the fact that the employer (government) is simultaneously the final maker of rules *and* a party to them. One obvious result has been the almost total prohibition of the right of public employees to strike in support of their bargaining demands. Labor relations in the public sector has thus been tempered by the inability of governments and unions to equalize their respective bargaining powers to the same extent as employers and unions in the private sector. One consequence of this imbalance is that public employees have occasionally engaged in illegal strikes as a way of expressing their frustration with a system so obviously rigged against them.

The wide variety of government employment, especially in terms of workplace technology, explains to a large extent the existence of different models of labor relations in the public sector. Some types of public employment, such as firefighting, are basically skilled occupations, prompting their associated unions to adopt craft-oriented organizational structures and strategies. Other areas of employment closely resemble the manufacturing sector, and the unions of these workers follow an industrial model of organization. In still others, for example, among teachers, the amalgamated model has been widely adopted.

The Role of Government in Collective Bargaining

Government is the third principal participant in the collective bargaining process. In this introductory section, the role of government in establishing and enforcing the legal framework of collective bargaining is emphasized. Subsequent sections will discuss the involvement of government and other agents in the substantive issues of collective bargaining.

All relationships between people and/or institutions involve rules or procedural assumptions which guide their behavior. In some cases the rules are formal, such as laws prohibiting criminal acts. In others, the rules are informal, such as those governing social or professional etiquette. Both kinds of rules are found in labor relations. Formal rules are found in the establishment of a legal framework within which collective bargaining can take place (the "rules for rule-making"). Informal rules are observed in the actual labor-management relationship, where workers/unions and owners/managers negotiate the various terms and conditions of employment.

The critical role of government in establishing and enforcing the "rules for rule-making" can be demonstrated through the different laws and legal interpretations that have been applied to workers and unions over the years. For example, before the passage of the Railway Labor Act in 1926, *no* American workers had a legal right to organize and bargain collectively with their employers. The National Labor Relations Act (1935) gave most private sector workers collective bargaining rights, but other large groups of workers, such as government employees and agricultural workers, were still excluded from coverage. Even those who are covered remain subject to a rigid set of rules governing the conduct of both unions and employers. Our constitutional form of government, in conjunction with the institutions of private property and capitalist economic organization, has determined not only *who* may bargain collectively but also *what* may be bargained over and *how* bargaining may be structured through public laws, decrees, and administrative/judicial decisions. The defeat of the proposed Labor Law Reform Act of 1977 and the changing posture of the NLRB should be strong reminders to those in the labor movement that their present rights remain precarious insofar as they are dependent upon the political process.

Union and Management Approaches to Collective Bargaining

It is usually individual workers in a given employment setting who initiate or attempt to initiate the collective bargaining process, but once established, collective bargaining is an organizational relationship between two representative groups: the union in behalf of the workers, and management in behalf of (or sometimes including) the actual owners of the enterprise.

The collective bargaining process can be characterized by a number of important elements. First, collective bargaining is not a single, once-and-for-all occurrence, like the negotiation between buyer and seller of the price for an automobile. Rather, collective bargaining is a continuing relationship involving both policy making and policy enforcement.

Second, collective bargaining is a process of consent and mutual accommodation between two representative groups with basically conflicting goals. Management seeks to maximize financial returns while, if necessary, remaining competitive. The union seeks to maximize the security and financial returns (wages and other economic benefits) of its members. Both parties, however, have a mutual interest in reaching a satisfactory agreement. As a result, collective bargaining is a changing mixture of conflict and cooperation; it is an exercise in the arts of power and persuasion.

Third, collective bargaining is a relationship of many dimensions which together comprise the core of the labor relations system. There is a significant economic component to the process, but there are many noneconomic considerations as well. In the course of negotiation, elements of conflict and cooperation are influenced by the uncertainties of having to establish a comprehensive framework of policies to govern future relations and to resolve future differences between the parties. Economic objectives, such as wages and fringe benefits may themselves be in conflict with noneconomic objectives, such as job security and the establishment of work rules.

Finally, collective bargaining has developed as a process which, to a significant degree, tends to blunt or replace competitive forces in the marketplace. Where there is no union or bargaining relationship, the employer can unilaterally decree wages and other conditions of employment, constrained or aided by the market forces of supply and demand. And while the same market forces exist where there is a bargaining relationship between labor and management, the bilateral establishment of terms for the purchase/sale of labor offers protection to workers from the impersonal, competitive operation of an otherwise unrestrained labor market.

Management Approach

Management's approach to collective bargaining is founded to a large extent on three basic operational objectives. First and foremost is the *profit motive* which has already been described in terms of its overriding importance to the typical business operation. It should be pointed out, however, that there are also areas of potential conflict within an enterprise—between owners/stockholders, who usually wish to maximize the dividend return on their investment, and managers, who are more often concerned with reinvestment for growth of the enterprise and/or their own personal gain. Thus, in collective bargaining, management is likely to consider business as well as personal objectives in seeking some combination of survival, growth, and profits.

The second objective involves *management rights*—that is, the desire to minimize worker/union encroachment on the overall latitude of owners/managers to direct production and the work force as they see fit in order to maintain efficient operations for the sake of survival, growth, and profits. For example, a union's efforts to reserve production work for only those union members classified to perform such tasks are a restriction on management's desire to maximize output regardless of the consequence to individual workers or groups of workers.

The third operational objective concerns the maintenance of a satisfactory work force—that is, the recruitment, training, and retention of workers with the skills and expertise necessary for production, and the organization of those workers in a manner which results in competitive productivity. Consequently, the *cost of labor* is but one of two primary considerations to management; the other is *output per worker*. Low-wage workers give a firm a competitive advantage only when their output per dollar of compensation is greater than that of higher-wage workers.

Although basic operational objectives have remained the same over the years, management philosophies have changed. Nineteenth-century labor relations was characterized by near-total control of workers by employers. In the early twentieth century, many employers experimented with "scientific management," where job content analysis and work measurement techniques were used in an attempt to increase the efficiency and satisfaction of workers. Between World War I and the Depression, the "American plan" called for labor-management cooperation based on patriotism. Employers felt that such an approach eliminated the need for outside (union) intervention in labor relations. Since the passage of federal labor legislation in the 1930s, employers have increasingly moved toward a human relations approach. This latter era has precipitated a phenomenal growth in the labor law and labor relations consultant industries. Even though management philosophies have apparently become less authoritarian over the years, employers have continued their adamant resistance to the unionization of workers.

Union Approach

The union's approach to collective bargaining is based on philosophical as well as operational objectives. Primary is the belief that collective bargaining is necessary to protect and promote the welfare of workers. The experience of American unions has been that neither employers nor the government will voluntarily protect workers from the oppressive forces of the marketplace and management's quest for production and profit.

On the economic front unions, through collective bargaining, seek to counteract impersonal market forces which can adversely affect the security of their members. In the sense of workplace government, unions attempt to assure the fair treatment of workers—to protect them from unreasonable management demands and to establish union-management procedures for resolving disputes between workers and employers.

American unions have developed a strong faith in collective bargaining as a process for peaceful decision making. As a result, unions and the labor movement as a whole have devoted much of their efforts to strengthening the union as a collective bargaining institution. As discussed in Chapter 4, union political activity, for example, has concentrated on achieving policies and programs to strengthen collective bargaining as the foundation of our labor relations system.

Initiating the Bargaining Process: When Workers Organize

In the building and construction industry, employers can legally take the initiative in establishing a collective bargaining relationship since the union hiring hall is their main source of potential employees. In most other areas of employment, however, it is either the workers seeking union representation or a union decision to organize a nonunion employer that marks the potential beginning of collective bargaining.

Industrial and public sector employees often join unions as a direct result of organizing campaigns at their individual places of employment. Most craft workers, however, are organized indirectly, as a consequence of entering joint apprenticeship programs that require union membership as a condition of continuing participation. Obviously, such programs provide work and training activities under an *existing* collective bargaining agreement.

In the final analysis, workers themselves must decide if they want union representation. When a union takes the initiative in organizing, the workers still have a choice of whether or not to join; even craft workers in effect *choose* union representation when they make the decision to enter a union-sponsored apprenticeship program.

Workers form and join unions for a variety of reasons. One principal reason is the desire for better wages and fringe benefits. Another is an interest in protection from unfair treatment and other forms of favoritism that management can exercise in the absence of a union's representational advocacy. A third reason workers join unions is for the social benefits of belonging to an organization that represents their interests on the job and provides an outlet for interpersonal relations and leadership aspirations. Where a union already has a collective bargaining agreement with an employer, new employees, after a probationary period agreed upon by the company and union, may be required to join the union which has negotiated their present benefits and which will represent them in the future.

The initial organizing campaign typically is designed around efforts to obtain signed "authorization cards" from as many eligible workers as possible. Organizationally, the goal is to build and maintain worker support until the employer recognizes the union as their representative for collective bargaining purposes. To accomplish this, most campaigns rely heavily on the establishment and operation of an effective inside (worker) committee with outside (union) support.

There are highly detailed and often controversial administrative (NLRB/FLRA) guidelines for judging the appropriateness of both union and employer conduct during organizing campaigns. For example, the union can emphasize the benefits to be gained from organizing but the employer is prohibited from promising additional benefits if the workers reject union representation. On the other hand, employers can make "captive audience" speeches against the union during working hours (except within 24 hours of a representation election) but legally deny the union a similar, paid-time forum for expressing its own views.

Overall, employers have a distinct advantage in the organizing process, in at least four important ways. First, employers are likely to have greater financial resources available for fighting the unionization of their workers. It is not unusual for "union avoidance" consultants to be paid several thousand dollars a day for their services. The union, on the other hand, typically must rely on limited paid staff and volunteers for its organizing efforts. Also to the employer's advantage is the matter of inertia. The employer's personnel administration and supervisory forces are already organized in the sense of knowing each other and working together for the goals of management. The workers, however, usually must start from scratch in building their own organization for union representation. Of course, the union is perceived as an "outside/unknown" factor in the eyes of management, and as such can be explained to the workers in terms of the employer's desire to resolve problems without the interference of a union. Third, and as mentioned in Chapter 3, time is almost always on the side of employers in an organizing campaign. The longer an employer can stall the workers' goal of union recognition, or a representation election, the better the chance that interest will fade—or that those still wanting a union can be replaced with "more reasonable" employees. Finally, the element of fear is a powerful employer tool for discouraging worker militancy in the form of union organizing. The fact that an employer can interrogate workers about their support of the union, so long as there are no threats of reprisal, can have a chilling effect on an organizing drive. Although it is clearly illegal to discriminate against or discharge workers for their union sentiments or activities, there are real disincentives for "pushing your luck," especially in times when alternative jobs are hard to come by.

Union Recognition

Before an actual bargaining relationship can be established, the employer must recognize the union as the representative of its employees. This may be accomplished either with or without government intervention.

If the workers want a particular union to represent them and the union can so convince their employer, the employer may voluntarily (that is, without government involvement) recognize the union and bargain with it. However, federal labor law severely restricts the right of most employees to strike and picket employers as a method of "convincing" them that they should voluntarily recognize their union. For instance, employees of a nonunion shop where no government-conducted election has been held in the preceding 12 months can strike and picket an employer for recognition no more than 30 days before a petition must be filed for an election to be conducted by the National Labor Relations Board. Where one union is already recognized or where there has been a valid NLRB election within a year, strikes, picketing, and election petitions are all outlawed for employees covered by the federal labor laws. Paradoxically, where workers are covered by neither federal nor state law (for example, agricultural laborers in some states), there is virtually unlimited freedom to strike and picket for union recognition. Such instances, however, are exceptional.

The overwhelming majority of employers refuse, for obvious reasons, to recognize unions voluntarily. In these and other situations where there may be a question of whether the union is actually desired by a majority of the employees or exactly which employees the union is entitled to represent, the matter is settled through a representation election conducted by a regional office of the NLRB. The NLRB regional office assigns a field examiner to establish the factual basis for an impending election, including:

(1) Whether the employer's operation is covered by federal law;
(2) Whether at least 30 percent of the employees have designated the union as their representative;
(3) Whether the appropriate employees have been included in the proposed bargaining unit; and
(4) Whether the petition has been properly filed.

If a factual basis for a representation election is established, the NLRB conducts a secret ballot election, usually within 30 days of a union's petition. The regional director of the Board then certifies the election results to the parties involved, stating the exact number of votes for and against union representation. If a union has been chosen by a majority of the employees, the Board will certify it as the official bargaining representative.

COLLECTIVE BARGAINING ISSUES AND PROCEDURES

Every employment relationship, whether union or nonunion, is based on what can be called a *wage and effort scale.* The wage scale is simply the level of pay per time unit worked; the effort scale involves the amount of work to be done in a given period of time. In addition, the terms of *individual security,* such as claims to available work, fair treatment on the job, promotion, layoff, recall, and discipline are fundamental to any employer-employee relationship.

In the absence of collective bargaining or some other form of employee participation, management unilaterally establishes the terms and conditions of individual security and the wage and effort scales, subject only to the forces of supply and demand in the marketplace and laws specifically regulating the employment of workers (such as equal employment opportunity, occupational safety and health, and minimum wage). Many employers can find workers who will accept employment without any voice in the determination of their wages and working conditions. Such employees are free to quit, of course, if they no longer want to work under such unilaterally established terms; alternatively, they can attempt to persuade their employer to include them in the decision-making process, usually by designating a union as their agent and representative.

Once a union is certified as the collective bargaining representative of a group of employees, the employer is required by law to bargain in good faith over various elements of the worker/union-employer relationship.[2] The law does not require the employer to agree to policies and procedures sought by the union. It provides only that the union must be given an opportunity to persuade the employer to agree to a mutually acceptable set of rules governing the employment relationship.

Where there is no union, the rules governing employment are often unwritten and largely implicit. Collective bargaining entails explicit rules which are customarily written in a collective bargaining agreement or, as it is usually called, a contract between the employer and the union.

Virtually every collective bargaining agreement includes provisions for wage and effort scales and individual security, both of which are basic to any employment relationship; the importance of collective bargaining, however, is that it requires the *bilateral* establishment of such terms. Collective bargaining agreements also typically contain provisions establishing the nature and scope of the relationship between the employer and the union as employee representative, namely: (1) questions of union security and management rights, and (2) the administration of the agreement, including a method for settling disputes over its meaning or application. Contract administration and dispute settlement are discussed in the fol-

[2]The legal concept of "good-faith bargaining" is discussed in Chapter 6.

lowing chapter. The three other basic areas of collective bargaining rulemaking are outlined below.

Wage and Effort Scales

Most of the public attention given to labor relations in the United States is focused on the economic aspects of collective bargaining, namely, wage and effort scales. Unions and employers may consider other basic areas of the labor-management relationship to be more important, but it is usually the economic issues that make the headlines. And to the typical worker, the clearest sign of the union's presence is its ability to secure good wages and working conditions for its members.

Before the widespread use of collective bargaining (which both contributed to and resulted from an increasing complexity of employer-employee relations), the wages paid workers and actual levels of effort in terms of productivity (output per worker hour) were fairly simple concepts which were therefore relatively easy to determine. Product and labor markets established the economic costs and benefits of employment and established trends which economists could use to predict economic behavior in the future.

Marginal Productivity Theory

Most economic analysis dealing with wage determination is based on *marginal productivity theory* which asserts that employers will continue to hire workers as long as they can profit from doing so—that is, to the point where the cost of additional labor exceeds the contribution that labor can make to revenues—and that employers seeking to maximize their profits will bid up wages to the value of the workers' contribution to output or production. Applying this theory to modern-day employment is difficult because it does not adequately explain situations where the forces of competition have been severely restricted. Marginal productivity theory assumes that both workers and employers freely compete in the marketplace for wage labor; but in fact, especially in the short run, most employers have relatively fixed labor requirements, and there are many barriers preventing workers from changing jobs solely on the basis of wage rates.

The practice of collective bargaining further limits the applicability of marginal productivity theory to wage and effort scale determination by introducing a new set of variables and a new concept of employment. When wages are fixed by negotiation rather than by the operation of market forces and/or the unilateral decisions of management, the basically economic framework of determination is broadened by a host of social and political considerations, especially from within the union. Thus collective bargaining may result in both financial and administrative barriers to the free operation of economic forces.

Theory of Negotiated Wages

Economists have thus moved from marginal productivity theory as the principal explanatory tool for wage determination toward what has been called a *theory of negotiated wages*, which, although imperfect itself, incorporates more of the realities of contemporary employer-employee relations. The main elements of this theory include:

(1) The influence of union politics and ethics;
(2) The possible substitution of nonwage items for wage items in the process of negotiations;
(3) Union pressures, such as a strike, which can broaden the types of conditions acceptable to an employer; and
(4) The effects of collective bargaining agreements which fix the level of wages for considerable periods of time.

Under collective bargaining, wages are part of a continuing, long-range relationship, so although bargaining is nearly always over wages to be paid in the future, both precedent and forecast may be relevant to labor-management negotiations. Thus, the principal wage criteria used in collective bargaining are:

(1) Wages paid for comparable work in the same or other industries;
(2) Changes in the cost-of-living (usually as indicated by the consumer price index);
(3) Changes in productivity at the plant or industry level; and
(4) The company's ability to pay, based on its recent profits or anticipated revenues.

Productivity is most closely associated with bargaining over effort scales so that, to the firm, wage costs are best expressed as *unit labor costs*, that is, the wages paid per unit of output. Thus, if productivity rises, workers can be paid proportionately higher wages without affecting a firm's unit labor costs. Negotiations over wages usually consider changes in productivity to assume a given level of effort by workers. An employer attempt to raise productivity by forcing workers to increase their level of effort, as opposed to introducing more efficient technology, is considered a "speedup" and will be opposed by the workers and the union. Thus wages and effort levels are inseparable issues in the bargaining process.

Wage criteria are useful for several reasons. They tend to make the process of negotiating from diverse and generally opposite positions more logical, and they serve to narrow the range of possible settlements. But, most of all, the application of wage criteria to the bargaining process allows both labor and management to justify the terms of any particular wage agreement.

Economic Supplements

The basic concepts of wage criteria also apply to the negotiation of *economic supplements* under collective bargaining. Such "fringe benefits" have become increasingly important in overall package settlements by labor and management. Prior to World War II, the economic issues addressed in collective bargaining were confined almost exclusively to wages and other forms of direct payment for work. But when wage controls were imposed during World War II, union negotiators were prompted to seek benefits indirectly, that is, in forms other than money wages. By the 1970s, many collective bargaining agreements included nonwage benefits amounting to nearly 40 percent of total economic costs (although the average for all contracts was around 25 percent).

The principal economic supplements that are now commonly found in labor-management agreements can be classified as:

(1) *Pay for time not worked* (vacations, holidays, sick leave, jury duty);

(2) *Premium pay* (overtime, shift work, holiday work); and

(3) *Welfare plans* (insurance, pensions, education, training allowances, legal services).

In recent years, numerous innovations have been bargained into welfare plans. For example, a growing number of contracts allow workers to choose "cafeteria style" from a variety of fringe benefits. Accordingly, plans can be tailored to individual needs within a given dollar limit. Also, there has been a trend toward single, year-end or profit-sharing bonuses tied to the economic health of the employer.

Government-mandated social insurance payments by an employer, such as workers' and unemployment compensation and social security premiums, represent an additional direct cost of employment. Thus, to the parties negotiating a contract, the total cost of all economic items is important. But the negotiating process itself is largely devoted to bargaining over the combination of wage and supplemental benefits desired by the union membership. Other direct labor costs and various wage criteria, especially comparability and the ability to pay, are important determinants of the economic package finally agreed upon.

Individual Security

To labor and management, the various noneconomic aspects of a collective bargaining agreement are often as important as wage and fringe benefits. The negotiation of individual security measures may be regarded as proof of this assertion. Historically, American unions have devoted considerable effort to gaining economic security for their members through collectively bargained protection of individual and group job rights. These efforts have been prompted by the decision that wage and supplemental benefits are of little value to workers if they face arbitrary management decisions regarding the allocation of work, promotion, transfer, layoff, recall, and discipline.

The union drive for job security, especially in the industrial sector, has been based on the principle of seniority, which holds that workers with the longest cumulative service have the greatest protection from layoff and thus receive the most benefits of employment. In some seasonal industries such as construction and garment manufacturing, unions have negotiated work-sharing arrangements instead of seniority provisions so that available work is distributed equally among their members.

The primary objective of both seniority and work sharing is the elimination of arbitrary management decisions on which workers will be laid off in case of a work force reduction. Without a negotiated procedure for layoff and recall, management is free to permanently furlough whichever employees it chooses, thereby gaining an opportunity to rid itself of "undesirable" employees (such as union sympathizers or older workers whose productivity may have fallen or who may soon be eligible for pension benefits). Likewise, in promotion or transfer, specific criteria for determining eligibility prevent favoritism or other subjective factors from influencing what should be objective processes of selection and placement.

There are reasons for both supporting and opposing union efforts to increase individual/job security through seniority and work-sharing provisions in collective bargaining agreements. Such provisions do eliminate favoritism and protect older workers. However, they also tend to penalize more productive workers, regardless of their length of service, and thus undermine management's ability to achieve maximum efficiency.

Placing the burden of work shortages on younger members (with less seniority) has been a source of division within the labor movement, tending to pit worker against worker, and seniority has occasionally been used against some minorities (for example, through the use of segregated rosters), but the practice certainly has more merits than drawbacks. Its scope has grown over the years to influence more than simply procedures for promotion, transfer, layoff, and recall. For example, wage and supplemental benefits may be tied to length of service and become more liberal as a worker accumulates seniority. The implications for bargaining are obvious; the exact nature of the seniority system will affect the cost of any economic item related to the length of service of covered employees.

Union Security and Management Rights

Fundamental to labor/management differences over the applicability of individual and group job security measures is the issue of management rights. The legal parties to a bargaining relationship are the union and the employer, not workers and managers. Collective bargaining is thus a test of power and authority between the union and the employer although, ultimately, it is workers and managers who carry out the process on a day-to-day basis.

At the heart of the conflict is the division of authority and thus control of the work environment. In the absence of a union, management is obviously the sole authority as long as business is conducted within the law. The presence of a union, however, forces management to share its authority since, once a union is legally recognized as the bargaining representative for a group of workers, the employer is required by law to negotiate with the union over wages, hours, and working conditions.

Predictably, employers and unions view the question of management rights quite differently. Employers have traditionally taken the position that management has an inherent right to direct the affairs of an enterprise. Any concession made to a union therefore decreases management rights, but any such rights not specifically conceded remain with the enterprise and its managers. Unions deny that employers have any *inherent* rights under collective bargaining and assert that management rights must be defined according to the particular labor-management relationship in each individual enterprise. Since the social and legal framework of collective bargaining is based on the principle of democratic self-determination for workers, it may be easier to understand the basic issues of the labor-management conflict from the union perspective.

Management has power and thus authority over workers because workers are dependent upon employers for money wages by which to survive and prosper. When workers organize into unions, this dependent relationship still exists, but the power and authority of managers over individual workers is decreased. The amount of this decrease is determined in the course of developing and continuing a collective bargaining relationship.

The negotiation of union security and management rights clauses is, therefore, basic to union and employer recognition of their mutual positions of power and authority. But since ownership and thus control (based on property rights) are vested with the employer, the union must take the initiative, not only in establishing its own security but also in restraining what management may claim as its inherent authority. The conflict is between labor's need to deal with employers from the strongest possible position and management's desire to retain as much unilateral control as possible over its operations.

Union security measures attempt to strengthen the position of the union beyond the rights guaranteed by exclusive recognition. Where there is no negotiated union security agreement, the labor-management relationship is referred to as an *open shop.* The union is legally bound to represent all workers in the bargaining unit, but workers are not required to be union members.

The strongest form of union security is the *closed shop,* where an employer can hire only workers who are already members of the union recognized as the exclusive bargaining agent. The Taft-Hartley Act outlawed this form of security in 1947, arguing that employers should have a free choice in whom they hire. The closed shop persisted, especially among the skilled trades, largely because employers needed dependable sources of labor and the closed shop served their needs. In 1959, the Landrum-Griffin Act exempted the construction industry from the Taft-Hartley 30-day minimum probation period before new employees could be required to become union members by substituting a seven-day minimum. Today, therefore, the closed shop continues for all practical purposes in the construction industry, although the wording of collective bargaining agreements is such as to remain within the letter of the law.[3]

The next strongest form of negotiated union security is the *union shop,* where the employer is required to make union membership a condition of continuing employment for all workers in the bargaining unit. New employees do not have to be union members when they are hired, but after a minimum of usually 30 days (the exact length of time is negotiated by the union and employer), they must join and remain members in good standing of the recognized union, or they can be discharged.

Two variations of the union shop are the *modified union shop,* where certain employee groups are exempted from union shop provisions, and the *maintenance of membership shop,* where, after an employee joins the union, he or she must remain a member in good standing for the duration of the collective bargaining agreement. Under maintenance of membership, there may also be a period (usually 15 days) at the beginning and end of the contract when workers in the bargaining unit can decide whether to join or remain in the union.

Section 14(b) of the Taft-Hartley Act permits individual states to outlaw the negotiation of union security clauses—that is, states may pass laws prohibiting collective bargaining agreements that make union membership a condition of continuing employment (so-called "right-to-work" laws). Thus it is proper to say that such laws create the *compulsory open shop* in which the union must represent everyone in the bargaining unit, but no one is compelled to belong to the union. Such situations show clearly why unions have fought so hard to negotiate the union security clauses where they are legal, and why the labor movement has continued its efforts to repeal Section 14(b). The necessarily weaker position of unions in states with compulsory open shop laws is evidenced by the common reference to such states as "right-to-work-for-less states." State-by-state wage statistics confirm the appropriateness of the reference.

Unions have attempted to achieve some form of union security in compulsory open shop states and other areas such as public employment where the law prohibits union security agreements through the negotiation, where legal, of *agency shop* recognition. In an agency shop, employees are not required to join the union, but

[3]Also in 1959, a court decision known as the *Mountain Pacific* case set forth procedures under which a hiring hall could legally function, namely, that referrals must be on a nondiscriminatory basis, without regard to union membership, and that an employer can reject any applicant referred by the union.

they must pay the union the equivalent of initiation fees and dues in the form of a "service charge" for their representation by the union.

Although not usually considered a form of union security, the negotiation of *dues checkoff,* that is, the payroll deduction of union dues for union members who have authorized the employer to do so, represents an administrative convenience for the union, which can strengthen its position by devoting time and resources otherwise spent on individual dues collections to other union business. Checkoff is now widespread, nearly always in conjunction with a union or agency-shop agreement. However, even where a union has checkoff but no further security other than exclusive recognition, the collection and lump sum payment of dues by the employer to the union is generally considered preferable to exclusive recognition alone.

The sections of a collective bargaining agreement covering union recognition, union security, and management rights are designed to answer several questions: who speaks for whom, with what power and authority, and with what exceptions? The first two questions are answered largely via statements of union recognition and security, although the power of the union depends ultimately on the strength and determination of its membership. The question of exceptions is the domain of management rights and represents the employer's effort to explicitly limit union encroachment on management's freedom to organize production with a minimum of worker interference or protest.

The Bargaining Process in Detail

Since the passage of the Wagner Act in 1935, legal and administrative decisions have defined all subjects for collective bargaining between labor and management as falling into one of three categories: mandatory, illegal, or voluntary. Mandatory items are those over which the parties must bargain in good faith if they are introduced by either side. Either party can bargain to the point of impasse over mandatory items, ultimately using economic weapons (strike or lockout) to enforce its position. Over the years, the National Labor Relations Board and the courts have consistently expanded the list of bargaining items held to be within the intention of the Act, and thus falling into the mandatory category. Since the law mandates bargaining over "wages, hours, and other terms and conditions of employment," such issues as vacation and holiday pay, insurance, piece rates, profit-sharing, and work schedules are obviously considered mandatory. "Other terms and conditions of employment" have increased over the years and now include such diverse topics as the duration of the agreement, rest and lunch periods, seniority, union security, plant and safety rules, no-strike clauses, and discipline and discharge procedures.

Illegal bargaining items are those forbidden by law, such as the closed shop or a union security clause in a state with a compulsory open-shop law. Such topics cannot be subject to bargaining, even if both parties agree; obviously, therefore, they cannot be included in a contract, since to do so would be in violation of the law.

Voluntary or "permissive" bargaining items refer to subjects that are neither mandatory nor illegal. Such topics may be proposed, but there is no obligation to bargain over them. Nor can either party bargain to impasse and then use economic weapons to support its claim to such items. An example of a voluntary bargaining item would be an employer's demand that the union poll its membership before calling a strike to enforce its position on mandatory bargaining items.

The main elements of the typical collective bargaining agreement therefore include both mandatory and voluntary bargaining items. The specific content of the agreement will be influenced primarily by the bargaining context of the market, workplace technology, power and influence of the parties, and the maturity of the bargaining relationship. Content will also depend on legal constraints, such as whether the workers are covered by federal or state law and whether the employer operates in the private or the public sector. Virtually every collective bargaining agreement covers the four basic areas of labor-management relations under bilateral negotiation:

(1) Wage and effort bargains,
(2) Individual security,
(3) Union security and management rights, and
(4) Contract administration and dispute settlement.

Comparison of Craft and Industrial Union Contracts

Because of the unique nature of the labor-management relationship from enterprise to enterprise and from industry to industry, no two collective bargaining agreements are exactly alike. However, a comparison of sample contracts from the two principal types of collective bargaining relationships reveals that while there are specific differences in content, the structure of most agreements is remarkably similar. Side-by-side analysis of the content of typical

Workers can be quite imaginative in getting their message across the picket line.

UAW Solidarity Magazine/Archives

Marine Draftsmen's Association members vote on a new contract offer at General Dynamics, Electric Boat Division.

UAW Solidarity Magazine/Mantyla

craft and industrial union contracts provides a basis for grasping their diversity while at the same time emphasizing the basic unity of purpose of all collective bargaining agreements.

Compared to industrial union contracts, craft union agreements are typically succinct in their coverage of the wage and effort bargain. The most striking difference between the two is found in their enumeration of wage scales. The craft agreement usually lists three or four basic rates, for journeymen, foremen, and apprentices (apprentice rates are generally graduated percentages of the journeyman rate, depending on time served). The industrial contract may contain hundreds of different job descriptions falling into a dozen or more pay grades. In addition, each pay grade may include length-of-service increments (based on the assumption that more experienced workers are more productive).

The effort bargain in craft agreements is often stated simply in terms of preserving the principles of the trade. Production standards are at the discretion of the craft worker, and management relies on the worker's skill and judgment to determine a fair day's work. In industrial union contracts, however, considerable attention may be given to the effort bargain. In addition, wage and effort scales may be directly linked together through piece rates, where industrial workers are paid (above some minimum) according to their actual production over some time period—a practice which would be most unusual for craft workers.

The provisions for premium pay (overtime, weekend work, holiday pay, etc.) are generally similar in craft and industrial contracts, largely because of their uniform coverage by fair labor standards legislation. However, craft agreements are generally more restrictive of management's right to require work other than what is regularly scheduled according to the terms of the contract.

Supplemental benefits such as insurance and pension plans are handled differently under craft and industrial contracts. Because craft workers typically work for numerous employers, their unions usually maintain their own benefit trust funds or participate in industrywide funds, both of which are supported by employer contributions. Industrial union contracts normally cover the employees of a given plant or company; therefore insurance and pension benefits can be established and administered by the employer, with the union as a monitoring agent.

The treatment of individual security in craft and industrial agreements is also easily contrasted because of differences in the organization of work and the union-employer relationship. Given the craft union's role as an agent for referring workers to employers, the typical craft union agreement is silent on the individual worker's claim to work. Job rights among craft workers are basically a matter of internal union rules which establish the procedures for referral. Once on the job, craft workers are guaranteed fair treatment by the usual contractual requirement that work reductions be shared equally. The independence and status of the craft worker are commonly recognized through the absence of particular language on matters of discipline and discharge.

Reflecting the more directly dependent relationship of industrial workers to their employers, industrial union contracts are generally far more detailed in their provisions for job security and the workers' right to fair treatment. Individual security for industrial union members has been gained largely through the negotiation of seniority provisions detailing the worker's claim to available work. Virtually every industrial union contract spells out procedures governing the promotion, transfer, layoff, and recall of workers in the bargaining unit. In addition, industrial contract language usually outlines specific procedures for discipline and discharge.

Since more and more craft union agreements are being negotiated with associations of numerous individual employers, the typical craft contract defines the bargaining unit according to a scope of work, detailing the exact nature of the jobs covered and the relationship of individual employers to the contract's signatory associations.

While the contract may make minimal reference to union security and management rights, this does not in any way mean that the parties to the agreement have disregarded or overlooked such important aspects of their relationship. On the contrary, largely as a result of very long-standing contractual relationships, craft unions and employers have developed an implicit understanding with regard to their respective roles and jurisdictions.

Union recognition is implicit in craft agreement provisions covering the hiring of workers. The contract may justify the creation and operation of a union hiring hall through its procedures requiring employers to notify the union of job vacancies and through the union's promise to refer qualified workers to employers. Until recently, the typical craft agreement did not contain dues checkoff as a form of union security or administrative aid. The organization of craft unions is such that members have traditionally paid their dues and initiation fees at the union hall to the business agent, who maintains the local's financial records as part of the job.

The issue of management rights is usually resolved via mutual recognition of the individual craft worker's skill and judgment. The traditions of the trade effectively preclude management encroachment on the craft worker's domain.

In contrast, the typical industrial union contract is far more explicit in regard to union security and management rights. The bargaining unit is carefully defined and states specifically which classifications of employees are included and excluded. In addition, the union is generally acknowledged as the exclusive representative of those workers in the bargaining unit with respect to wages, hours, and other terms and conditions of employment. If a form of union security has been negotiated, its exact structure will be stated, along with any provision for dues checkoff.

Most industrial union contracts also contain specific language covering management rights. The provision may state simply that all matters not explicitly recognized as subject to union discretion remain the exclusive jurisdiction of the company, or a very detailed enumeration may be made of management activities which are exclusive company rights.

Contract administration and dispute settlement provisions of the typical craft and industrial union contracts also reflect the difference in the labor relations contexts of these two basic types of collective bargaining relationships. With constantly changing work crews on craft jobs, the business agent is the person most likely to maintain a long-range and maturing relationship with a given employer. Therefore, in most craft settings, the steward is the appointed representative of the business agent, who intervenes if management does not satisfactorily correct a problem called to its attention by the steward. In industrial settings, however, continuing contact between workers and managers provides the opportunity to develop dispute-settlement procedures that can directly involve the workers.

In grievance and arbitration procedures as well, craft and industrial union practices reflect the differences in their respective bargaining contexts. These differences and the resultant practices will be discussed in greater detail in the following chapter. In general, however, industrial union bargaining usually leads to more complex and hierarchical provisions than those in craft bargaining.

Factors That Affect the Content and Outcome of Collective Bargaining

Before turning to a discussion of the bargaining process itself, it will be helpful to review some broad categories of factors which, in addition to the bargaining contexts discussed above, tend to affect the content and outcome of collective bargaining. There are generally six such categories, three of which can be considered internal to the bargaining process and three external.

To the extent that they establish a framework or otherwise define the boundaries of the collective bargaining process, laws and government policies are *internal* to labor-management negotiations. Such laws and policies are established prior to the initiation of the bargaining process and certainly influence its outcome, because they regulate strikes, boycotts, and jurisdictional disputes, prohibit the negotiation of forbidden (illegal) items, and enable strikers to receive unemployment benefits and employers to limit wage offers to government-established wage guidelines or controls.

A second group of factors internal to collective bargaining involves the strength and attitude of the employer in the bargaining process. Obviously the economic position of the employer can be crucial to the outcome of negotiations. But the company's attitude (does it accept its bargaining responsibility or is it simply waiting for a chance to destroy the union?) is often an equally important, if not more important, consideration as documented by the experience of PATCO in 1981 and Continental Airline employees in 1982.

The strength and attitude of the union, both locally and nationally, constitute the third category of internal factors in the bargaining process. Many considerations together determine the overall position of the union relative to the company in bargaining. How long has the union been established? How long has the union represented the workers of the particular employer? What is the financial strength of the treasury of the local and the international? Is there a strike fund? What is the attitude of the union members toward the employer and toward the union leadership?

The nature of the geographic area and of the industry are factors *external* to the bargaining process. The content and outcome of negotiations are likely to be influenced by the average wage in the industry, the average wage in the community, wages paid by the employer's principal competitors, the extent of union organization in the community and in the industry, and the economic composition of the area in which bargaining takes place.

Community attitudes are also external factors and are closely related to considerations of geographic area and industry. Labor-management negotiations are almost certainly affected by such factors as the attitude of the community toward unions in general and the union in particular; the number of workers in the community represented by the union; the relationships of various unions in the community; and the influence and prestige of both management and union leaders in the community.

General economic trends in the area and the nation comprise the third category of external factors. The most significant considerations will probably include recent wage and price trends both locally and nationally, recent bargaining settlements both locally and nationally in the same and other industries, and local, regional, and national levels of unemployment.

These internal and external factors, together with the influence of bargaining contexts, determine the structural framework of collective bargaining. The role of government is particularly important because of its influence in the definition of appropriate bargaining units. As mentioned above, when a petition for a representation election is filed with the NLRB, one of the questions that must be answered prior to voting is exactly which workers are to be included in the proposed collective bargaining relationship.

As a rule, if the employer and the union agree on the workers to be covered, the NLRB will abide by their decision. However, if there is a dispute over the appropriate bargaining unit, the Board must make the determination. In doing so, the Board considers the nature of the industry, its product and labor markets, the mutuality of interests between workers and employers, and, perhaps most important, the previous history of labor relations—in particular, the relative equality of union and employer bargaining power. As a result, numerous types of bargaining structures have evolved over the years.

In the 1970s, about 80 percent of all collective bargaining agreements covered employees of a single enterprise; some two thirds were limited to a particular job site. But the number of workers covered by agreements involving more than one employer and/or more than one union had been growing for a number of years. At the local level, multiemployer agreements were and still are commonly found in the construction, retail trade, and publishing industries; at the regional level, such contracts had been negotiated in the longshore and maritime industries. While it was relatively uncommon to negotiate contracts in their entirety on an industry/national level, this was occasionally done, as in the glass container industry.

More often, in major industries such as steel and auto, a combination of individual plant and industrywide bargaining had developed. Major economic items such as wages and supplemental benefits were negotiated at the industry level, while local issues such as work rules and practices were negotiated at the job site.

However, such efforts at coordinated bargaining on the part of both labor and management fell into disfavor in the late 1970s and early 1980s, largely at the insistence of employers. A combination of changing economic circumstance and political climate prompted employer initiatives to reverse a long-run trend toward multiemployer, multiplant bargaining. For example, Chrysler's misfortunes turned "big three" into "big two" bargaining in 1979 and in 1986, for the first time in 40 years, the major steelmakers each negotiated individually with the United Steelworkers. The question remaining is whether better economic times and a recovered labor movement can reverse the current growth of segmented and increasingly localized bargaining. The answer likely will depend on both union and management responses to the changing contexts of labor relations in a dynamic and unpredictable economy.

Collective Bargaining: Preparation and Negotiation

Collective bargaining is a complex and intricate undertaking because of the many institutional considerations, both internal and external, which affect the process. We have already discussed the various labor relations contexts, the basic types of collective bargaining relationships, and other internal and external factors which may influence the content and outcome of labor-management negotiations. The actual process of contract negotiations, however, involves a relatively simple concept—that of two opposing parties bargaining to mutually acceptable agreement.

For those under its jurisdiction, federal labor law requires that the party wishing to modify or terminate an existing collective bargaining agreement must notify the other party in writing at least 60 days before the contract expiration and must notify the Federal Mediation and Conciliation Service and any similar state agency within 30 days of that notification, provided no agreement has been reached. The law recognizes that although preparations for contract negotiations may have been under way for some time (often over the entire life of the agreement), the actual bargaining usually takes place within the last few weeks or months of a contract's date of termination.

The overwhelming majority of labor-management agreements are consummated without resort to the use of economic weapons; that is, the ending of one contract is usually followed immediately by the beginning of another. Thus, compared to contract *administration* (the policy enforcement phase of labor relations), which continues over the entire life of an agreement, the time devoted by unions and management to contract *negotiations* (the policy enactment phase) is a brief, although usually intense, period in the overall bargaining process.

Although in recent years employers have increasingly taken the offensive by initiating bargaining demands of their own (in the form of "take-backs," i.e., trying to reverse the previous gains of workers), the union still typically serves notice that it wants to continue or modify its collective bargaining agreement with an employer. This is because once the union has been recognized and a contract has been negotiated, some initiative is necessary to perpetuate a collective bargaining relationship between a union and an employer; otherwise, with the expiration of the contract, the contractual relationship would cease to exist. Since the union is usually the initiating party and since both unions and companies prepare for negotiations in generally similar ways, we can describe the activities involved by looking at what the typical union must do before it goes to the bargaining table, if it wants to realize the maximum possible improvements for its members.

Every local union, whether negotiating its first or thirty-first contract with an employer, should rely heavily on its most direct source of information for contract proposals: its members. They, of course, are the reason for establishing or continuing a collective bargaining relationship, and they alone are in daily contact with the issues and problems for which policy is to be established at the bargaining table. The union's other direct source of information is its own experience with the employer, especially as manifested in the types of grievances filed and whether they were won or lost. Such issues can determine bargaining demands and priorities. In addition, the union has a variety of other sources of information in preparing for negotiations. Information is available from the international, from other unions, and from government agencies regarding the many internal and external factors which may influence bargaining demands.

Ideally the union's bargaining proposals will be based on a number of considerations, some as a result of information gathered, others depending on its intended bargaining strategy. Once the union has outlined its principal contract objectives according to the needs and desires of the membership, it must decide how to present them and negotiate a contract in the most advantageous manner. This decision will be based in large part on the context of the bargaining relationship. For example, in some labor-management relationships bargaining is conducted on the assumption that both parties come into negotiations with highly inflated demands, fully expecting to bargain from their respective extreme positions to a more moderate settlement. In others, past experience tells the negotiators that there is very little "fat to be trimmed" during the negotiating process.

In labor relations contexts where negotiations are conducted from opposite extremes, bargaining is likely to be based largely on the strategy of timely *counterproposals*; in situations where negotiations begin on a more realistic note, the tendency is toward *trading* one demand for another. Thus, the initial union proposals are likely to be influenced by the form of bargaining expected to take place. Regardless of its original position, however, the union must decide the final terms of agreement which it will accept and what combination of counterproposals and trading can be factually justified both to management during negotiations and to the membership for ratification.

The selection of negotiators also depends on the labor relations context and/or sometimes on the particular issues being negotiated. The membership of the union is best served by the most representative committee possible. The person who will speak for the committee as a whole should be especially respected throughout the union's diverse membership (young/old, white/nonwhite, male/female, skilled/unskilled, etc.).

Negotiations usually begin on a formal and sometimes theatrical note, attended by numerous official interested parties from both sides and, occasionally, representatives of the media. This initial stage of the bargaining process therefore is typically devoted to introductions, agreement on procedures and time schedules, and the presentation of written proposals. Such preliminaries are essential in setting the stage for serious discussions to come and in permitting the negotiating teams to initially assess each other's bargaining style.

The logical next step in describing the bargaining process in detail would be to elaborate on exactly what the typical, experienced negotiating committee does, step by step, to achieve its intended objectives. But such an attempt would be analogous to seeking step-by-step directions for painting a masterpiece or composing a classic opera. Collective bargaining is an art, not a science. The best way to learn the art of negotiating is to become thoroughly familiar with its techniques and procedures and then rely on ability and experience to produce the best possible results.

The procedures of the negotiating process can be classified according to the steps typically required to get from presentation of demands to final acceptance of a new contract. The initial proposals are generally followed by a period of mutual exploration and sorting out of priorities by both parties. This process, for both sides and by each side, may be conducted through a general discussion of problems or by the proposal, in outline form, of specific contract language.

Once they have a good idea of issues and priorities, experienced negotiators will quickly begin to look for ways to demonstrate that progress can be and is being made. This is often done by attempting to resolve minor issues first, thus developing momentum and confidence for tackling more critical and less easily agreed-upon areas of difference. And the negotiators must always remember that they must design an acceptable package covering the four bargaining functions—(1) wage and effort scales, (2) individual and job security, (3) union security and management rights, and (4) contract administration.

This is where technique comes into play, resulting in a more or less artistic approach to achieving final agreement in the form of a written contract. As negotiations progress, at whatever pace, the existence of a deadline in the form of an impending union strike or an employer lockout emphasizes the seriousness of actions taken or contemplated. Both technique and procedure become increasingly sensitive to individual personalities. The negotiators' patience, fairness, and integrity are subjected to the pressures of a deadline for either reaching agreement or facing a work stoppage—thus, the critical role played by the strike and the lockout as economic weapons in the collective bargaining process. Since strikes and lockouts are harsh and undesirable consequences of the failure to reach agreement, the possibility of their being used in the absence of a timely settlement forces the negotiating parties to reassess their positions, to look for new areas of compromise, and to try to accommodate each other; otherwise they must in effect quit negotiating and start preparing for economic warfare.

The power of the threat of strike or lockout in prompting labor and management adversaries to reach timely settlements is demonstrated by the fact that each year, on the average, less than one fourth of one percent of total available working time in the United States is lost through work stoppages resulting from the collective bargaining process. The losses from a strike or a lockout are potentially great, but most observers agree that, for society as a whole, the price of maintaining workers' freedom to withhold their labor pending bilateral (union-management) agreement on the terms and conditions of their employment has indeed been a small one to pay.

Developments and Evolving Techniques in Collective Bargaining

Since the passage of the Wagner Act in the 1930s, the proportion of collective bargaining agreements negotiated and ratified by union memberships without the occurrence of a union strike or an employer lockout has risen steadily.[4] This trend has led some observers to conclude that labor and management have been steadily moving closer together, to a more central ground of accommodation and cooperation; some feel this accommodation has been to the overall detriment of the best interests of workers. Many feel simply that time has prompted a maturing of labor relations which has been beneficial to companies, unions, and workers alike.

A third, more factual explanation of decreasing labor-management strife in recent decades is that many of the issues which were once major causes of economic warfare between unions and companies are settled by law or by government regulation. Questions of union recognition, bargaining unit determination, and unfair collective bargaining practices, for example, are now resolved largely through established administrative procedures. In addition, most workers today have legal rights and protection for minimum wages, hours, overtime, industrial safety and health, and many other such employment-related issues for which their predecessors had to bargain or strike.

Post-Vietnam-era labor relations involved a fourth element of "stability"— one that has been unsettling to workers and unions as well as to proponents of collective bargaining itself. The economic turmoil of the 1970s and 1980s in combination with deteriorating legal protections—especially following the defeat of labor law reform—served to put employers on the offense and the labor movement on the defense. Without question, the cumulative effects of plant closings, mass layoffs, the wholesale firing/replacement of strikers, and the over-all climate of concession bargaining made workers and unions less willing to assume the risks of economic warfare with employers. These developments have led some within management to suggest that collective bargaining no longer serves a useful purpose in our society. Unions and their supporters, of course, bitterly contest this notion.

By the mid-1980s, there were some sectors of the economy and geographic areas of the country where the overall environment for labor relations appeared similar to that faced by the majority of

[4]There were fewer major strikes and lockouts in 1985 than anytime since the U.S. Department of Labor began keeping such statistics in 1947.

American workers in the 1930s. And today, there may be a few long-standing labor-management relationships where unions and companies have seemingly moved too close together for the best interests of the workers. But in the majority of labor relations settings, there remains strong evidence that, while maintaining their traditional adversary roles, labor and management have found new and more effective ways to utilize collective bargaining to their mutual benefit.

As a result of the recognition that collective bargaining has become a permanent part—in fact, the foundation—of the American labor relations system, unions and management have expanded its scope (for the most part at union urging) to cover an ever-widening range of issues and problems related to the four basic bargaining functions. This expansion can easily be demonstrated by comparing a typical pre-World War II contract to one of today. Especially in terms of wage and effort provisions (notably fringe benefits) and individual security, contemporary collective bargaining agreements are far more encompassing than those of only a few decades ago.

In addition, the expanded scope of collective bargaining and the growing experience and expertise of its participants have led unions and employers to seek alternatives to the use of their respective economic weapons, since these weapons have such mutually devastating consequences. In principle, collective bargaining is designed to be a rational and constructive process. However, if strikes and lockouts are considered to be *necessary* to bargaining rather than facilitative in promoting agreement, the collective bargaining environment tends to become irrational and destructive. Collective bargaining authority David Cole has distinguished these two opposing viewpoints succinctly:

> To suggest that we cannot have collective bargaining without reliance directly on the strike as the moving force is like saying that, in international relations, if we renounce warfare we cannot have diplomacy. In both situations, precisely the contrary is true.[5]

Thus, to a great degree, labor and management (both together and separately) have sought to strengthen the rational and constructive aspects of the collective bargaining environment. Labor has moved to reduce strikes resulting from jurisdictional disputes and raiding, for example, through the AFL-CIO's Procedure for Determining Organizing Responsibilities, and the Internal Dis-

[5]David L. Cole, "Focus on Bargaining: The Evolving Techniques," *American Federationist* (May, 1974).

Key Words and Phrases

agency shop
American Plan
amalgamated model of industry/union organization for collective bargaining
authorization card
automation technology
bargaining by trading demands
bargaining as an art, not a science
bargaining priorities
bargaining proposals
bargaining strategy
bargaining unit
bargaining via counter-proposals
bilateral decision making
cafeteria style benefits
captive audience speech
closed shop
collective bargaining agreement
compulsory open shop
consumer price index
cost of living
craft model of industry/union organization of collective bargaining
division of labor
exclusive representation
Federal Mediation and Conciliation Service
fringe benefits
good-faith bargaining
handicraft technology
illegal bargaining subjects
individual security
industrial model of industry; union organization for collective bargaining
job security
labor relations contexts
labor relations system
maintenance of membership shop
management rights
mandatory bargaining subjects
marginal productivity theory
mass production technology
modified union shop
open shop
package settlement
permissive or voluntary bargaining subjects
representation election
rules for rule making
scientific management
seniority
skilled labor as a direct factor of production
skill versus expertise in the nature and content of work
sovereignty
speedup
strike versus lockout
sunset laws
supplemental benefits
"take-back" in bargaining
terms and conditions of employment
theory of negotiated wages
unilateral decision making
union hiring hall
union recognition
union security
union shop
unit labor costs
wage and effort scale
wage criteria

putes Plan which effectively prohibits unwanted competition among its affiliates. Most advances, however, have resulted from joint union-management efforts to facilitate agreement without resorting to the use of economic sanctions. Some notable developments include:

(1) The use of prenegotiation conferences to shape and clarify the issues and content of negotiations;
(2) Joint labor-management designation of outside specialists to develop agreed-upon factual bargaining data;
(3) The establishment of joint study committees for periodic or continuing review of vital issues; and
(4) Advance agreement to submit unsettled contract issues to arbitration.

In addition, labor and management are increasingly using the mediation and conciliation services of government and private parties to assist in cases of impasse (where the union and employer cannot reach agreement on their own). Although such a move might be considered an indication of decreased confidence in the ability of the principal negotiating parties to reach agreement without third-party assistance, another explanation is simply that both labor and management have become more willing to explore all possible avenues for peaceful settlement before turning to economic warfare as their last resort.

At the same time, however, unions and employers alike have maintained strong opposition to structured intervention in the bargaining process, either by government seizure of an industry as allowed by federal law in "national emergency disputes" or through the compulsory arbitration of unsettled collective bargaining issues. If one leg of the American labor relations system is the right to strike, the other is just as surely the principle of voluntarism. The rights of strike and lockout encourage labor and management to try to agree. Voluntarism assures that even with serious consequences for failure to agree, the parties retain the right not to agree.

Review and Discussion Questions

1. Review the major historical periods in the development of collective bargaining in the United States, and contrast them, where appropriate, using Dunlop's three institutional contexts of the labor relations system.

2. Compare and contrast union/industry organization for collective bargaining under handicraft and mass production technologies.

3. In what ways does government influence the form, content, and outcome of collective bargaining in the United States?

4. Review the principal union and management objectives in the collective bargaining process. What are the major differences between union and nonunion worker-employer relationships?

5. Review and discuss the various wage criteria used in collective bargaining. Do you think that the relative importance of each criterion might vary from industry to industry? If so, why and in what ways?

6. Describe the principal forms of union security negotiated by American unions, and classify them according to their past and present legality in different states of the nation. Is the issue of union security still such an important one in this country? If so, why?

7. Compare and contrast typical craft and industrial union collective bargaining agreements according to the four basic bargaining functions. What factors are most responsible for their similarities and their differences?

8. Relate the various internal and external factors which affect the content and outcome of collective bargaining to the contention that, in negotiations, successful strategy depends on thorough preparation.

9. Identify the basic types of collective bargaining structures found in the American labor relations system. What determines the type of bargaining structure adopted by a particular industry or union?

10. Discuss the basis and meaning of the assertion that negotiating is an art, not a science. In what ways have recent developments in collective bargaining made this less true today than in the 1930s and 1940s?

11. Name several ways in which the existence of a strike/lockout deadline can facilitate reaching agreement under collective bargaining. From your reasons, does it follow that collective bargaining could not work without the rights of strike and lockout?

12. Unions and employers as a whole remain adamantly opposed to compulsory third-party arbitration of unsettled issues in contract negotiations; yet at the same time, they are increasingly using mediation and conciliation services and other outside resources when a bargaining impasse is reached. What is the explanation for this apparent contradiction in labor-management relations?

Chapter Resources and Suggested Further Reading

Complete bibliographical information for the following titles can be found in the Bibliography.

Beal, Wickersham, and Kienast, *The Practice of Collective Bargaining.*

Craypo, *The Economics of Collective Bargaining: Case Studies in the Private Sector.*

Marshall, Briggs, and King, *Labor Economics, 5th Edition.*

Richardson, *Collective Bargaining by Objectives.*

Schlossberg and Sherman, *Organizing and the Law.*
Slaughter, *Concessions and How to Beat Them.*

Collective bargaining and contract negotiations:

Bloom and Northrup, "Organizing and Negotiating," in *Economics of Labor.*
Butler, "The Nature of Collective Bargaining," in *Labor Economics and Institutions.*
Cohen, "The Participants and the Process" and "The Bargaining Contract," in *Labor in the United States.*
Lester, *Economics of Labor.*
Marshall, Cartter, and King, "Collective Bargaining and Economic Issues," in *Labor Economics.*
Sloane and Witney, "At the Bargaining Table," in *Labor Relations.*

Bargaining issues and developments in particular industries:

Chamberlain, Neil W., "Determinants of Collective Bargaining Structure," in *The Structure of Collective Bargaining,* edited by Weber.
Chandler, Margaret K., "Craft Bargaining," in *Frontiers of Collective Bargaining,* by Dunlop & Chamberlain.
Dunlop, John T., "The Industrial Relations System in Construction," in *The Structure of Collective Bargaining,* edited by Weber.

Maybe they call it "take-home pay" because there is no other place you can afford to go with it.

—Franklin P. Jones, 1953

Our labor unions are not narrow, self-seeking groups. They have raised wages, shortened hours, and provided supplemental benefits. Through collective bargaining and grievance procedures, they have brought justice and democracy to the shop floor.

—John F. Kennedy, 1962

To each laborer, the whole product of his labor, or as nearly as possible, is a most worthy object of any good government.

—Abraham Lincoln, 1847

6

Collective Bargaining: Contract Administration*

. . . grievance machinery under a collective bargaining agreement is at the very heart of the system of industrial self-government.

—Justice William O. Douglas (1960)

Chapter 5 discussed the process of collective bargaining, with particular reference to the *negotiation* of labor-management agreements. This chapter covers the *administration* of collective bargaining agreements, emphasizing dispute settlement as one of the four basic functions of bargaining under bilateral, union-management decision making.

Collective bargaining in labor relations has often been described as a system of industrial jurisprudence, which implies not only policy enactment (negotiations) but also policy enforcement (administration and dispute settlement). Obviously, in a democracy, it is meaningless to have laws without the means to guarantee their full application and to resolve questions about their interpretation. Accordingly, contract administration should be considered as important as contract negotiation in the maintenance of a viable labor relations system.

To workers and their unions, fair representation depends first on the negotiation of basic rules governing wage and effort scales, individual security, and union security. But the realization of the purpose and benefits of these rules actually hinges on the assurance

*This chapter is based largely on the writings of Richardson; Sloane and Witney; and various public documents. See Chapter Resources and Bibliography for specific references.

of their full and fair application. In short, even the best contract is relatively useless unless some mechanism exists for enforcing its provisions on a day-to-day basis at the workplace.

Defining the Process

The interdependence of policy enactment and policy enforcement has been recognized throughout the history of collective bargaining. Federal law explicitly states that as part of the bargaining process employees have the right to present grievances to their employers. In addition, the federal courts have ruled that even in those rare cases where a collective bargaining agreement does not include a formal grievance procedure, workers still retain the right to grieve over their wages, hours, and other terms and conditions of employment.

Since collective bargaining agreements cover the basic issues arising from the worker/union-employer relationship, it is logical to assume that a contract's grievance procedure should provide for the settlement of virtually all disputes deriving from that relationship. Thus, broadly defined, a grievance is any dispute between workers/unions and employers regarding their respective rights as established by law, the contract, or past practice. The grievance process is designed primarily to protect the rights of workers, namely, their negotiated wage and effort scales, matters of individual security, and the guarantee of fair treatment both on the job and in the resolution of work-related disputes with their employers. The grievance process does *not* exist to settle disputes among workers, between a worker and a union, or between unions; by definition, the bilateral nature of collective bargaining confines dispute settlement to issues arising from the employment relationship.

As a representative party to the employment relationship, the union is an additional actor in the grievance process. Especially in those areas where the union's interests are primary (such as union security and equal representation of the entire bargaining unit), the union may be the grieving party.

Rarely does an employer initiate a grievance. Given the legal protections afforded property ownership and its accompanying rights of "direction and disposal," the burden of proof in labor-management disputes typically lies with the workers and their union. The very existence of a grievance procedure implies that employers can act on their own behalf in directing and managing a work force. The most important exceptions to this rule involve matters of discipline and discharge, where, as in legal proceedings, a worker is considered innocent until proven guilty and management must prove that discipline or discharge was for "just cause."

The Grievance Procedure and Why It Works

Because collective bargaining agreements are negotiated by employers and unions rather than by individual managers and individual workers, a grievance legally exists between the *company* and the *union*, even though an individual worker may be its subject. This is consistent with the fundamental intent of collective bargaining: Individual workers have an organization to represent them on an equal basis with the organization of their employer.

Just as individual workers are generally powerless relative to their employer in the negotiation of wages and other terms and conditions of employment, they are likewise disadvantaged in the settlement of work-related disputes. This important principle of labor relations can be illustrated by contrasting the communications process under typical nonunion and union conditions (see Figure 2).

Under nonunion conditions, communication and decision making between workers and their employers are at the discretion of management; the terms of employment are unilaterally determined in the absence of collective bargaining. The presence of a union, with a hierarchical organization similar to that of the employer, changes one-way communication into two-way (bilateral) communication, giving the workers an effective voice through their own representatives, who are the legal equals of their management counterparts in the collective bargaining process. Bilateral communication and decision making create an environment in which collective bargaining can facilitate the administration of labor-management agreements, especially through the use of established grievance machinery.

In spite of wide variations in specific content and procedure from contract to contract, a number of important principles are embodied in virtually every grievance procedure. One important principle is the *right* of workers to grieve, either individually or collectively, through the union as their representative. Although Section 9 (a) of the National Labor Relations Act provides in part that individual employees "shall have the right at any time to present grievances to their employer and to have such grievances adjusted, without the intervention of the bargaining representative," the individual worker has greater protection as well as a stronger bar-

Last stop on Henry Ford's final assembly line. Highland Park, Mich., 1913. *Archives of Labor and Urban Affairs, Wayne State University*

Thousands of sympathizers supported the New Orleans streetcar strike of 1929. *Archives of Labor and Urban Affairs, Wayne State University*

gaining position when grieving through the union. Obviously, a union which has the backing of its membership is in a bargaining position superior to that of an individual employee or group of employees. In addition, as illustrated by Figure 2, union representatives hold a position of equality with employer representatives which is unattainable by workers.

For example, a worker, even though a union member, could be fired for insubordination if he or she used extremely profane language in arguing with a supervisor over a grievance. However, the same profane conduct on the part of a union representative (although perhaps unbecoming) could not result in dismissal, because the union representative is legally an equal of the management representative, and as a result no superior-subordinate relationship exists.

A second important principle in the grievance process is the recognition that it is preferable to resolve worker-employer disputes *directly*. Therefore, representatives of higher levels of authority (both union and management) should become involved only when the principal parties are unable to reach agreement. Thus the typical contract grievance procedure calls for disputes to be initiated by the worker(s) and presented to the immediate supervisor. If no settlement is reached, the grievance is then referred to successively higher levels in the bargaining process (see Figure 2), until a settlement is finally reached.

The third principle involved in the grievance process is the *timely and orderly* resolution of grievances without interruption of work. This principle is implemented in two ways in the typical collective bargaining agreement. First, the parties set time limits for each of the successive steps in the grievance procedure, for both initiation of the grievance and response to it. These deadlines prevent grievances from becoming "stale" and preclude stalling by either party. Second, there is an agreed-upon point of termination for every dispute (usually arbitration). This encourages prompt settlement so as to avoid the time, expense, and other consequences of bargaining to impasse.

The final principle in the grievance process is the practice of reducing disputes to writing. This is done for the same reasons of formal bargaining and record keeping that have already been mentioned regarding contract negotiations. Written grievances clarify the issues at hand and establish a factual record of bargaining settlements.

Collective Bargaining Law and Contract Administration

Collective bargaining as a continuous process in labor relations is perhaps best demonstrated by the traditional application of labor law to both contract negotiations and contract administration. Virtually all federal and state labor legislation for both private and public employment emphasizes the inseparable nature of policy enactment and policy enforcement. Chapter 3 discussed the legal concepts of exclusive representation and fair representation as they apply both to the negotiation and to the administration of collective bargaining agreements.[1] Two additional important legal concepts should be mentioned as well.

The concept of *good-faith bargaining* has been basic to the legal framework of labor relations since the passage of the Wagner Act in 1935. The duty of employers and unions to bargain is enforceable under the unfair labor practice provisions of the Act. But the law specifically states in Section 8(d) that "such obligation does not compel either party to agree to a proposal or require the making of a concession," a clear reminder of the voluntary nature of bargaining as well as the intention that its substance be free of governmental interference.

The question of good faith arises directly from the parties' duty to bargain—but within a framework of voluntary agreement. The law requires that the union and the employer meet, make their proposals, state their objections to each other's proposals and the reasons therefor, and then in good faith seek to narrow their differences and ultimately reach agreement. But good faith is a state of mind which is difficult to measure; thus the NLRB and the courts have decreed that certain kinds of conduct in the collective bargaining relationship are violations of the duty to bargain, regardless of the question of good faith. Known as *per se* violations, such acts as refusing to meet, refusing to sign a written contract, and unilaterally changing wages or working conditions are considered refusals to bargain in themselves and are therefore necessarily classified as unfair labor practices.

In the majority of refusal-to-bargain cases, the "totality of conduct" is judged rather than a single act. For example, even though an employer might appear to have engaged in extensive bargaining with a union, the record as a whole may indicate an attempt to frus-

[1]The reader is urged to review related sections in Chapter 3, especially pages 67–69.

trate or disrupt negotiations and to deny the union's right to joint decision making.

The other legal foundation of collective bargaining (one which is especially relevant to contract administration) is the continuous duty to furnish relevant information. This obligation, whose refusal is also a *per se* violation of NLRA unfair labor practice provisions, has been firmly established by arbitrators, the NLRB, and the courts. The duty to furnish information applies equally to unions and employers, and is based on the premise that intelligent and rational bargaining can proceed only from factual information relating to the subjects at issue.

Disputes over the provision of information for bargaining usually originate with unions, since they typically possess little employment data that is not equally accessible to employers. Some information, however, can be provided only by employers.

This problem is as prevalent in contract administration as it is in contract negotiation. For example, the union may need production data over the life of its current contract to prepare and defend its proposals for wage increases under a new collective bargaining agreement. At the same time, the union could be processing a grievance for a worker who received a disciplinary warning for failing to meet a production quota; the union might therefore request production records for the grievant and for other workers doing the same job. The employer's refusal to supply such information would be an obvious denial of the union's right to the factual data necessary for bargaining either the new contract or the settlement of the grievance under the existing contract; with such a refusal, the employer would be guilty of bad-faith bargaining.

Impasse Resolution: The Terminal Point in Dispute Settlement

Chapter 5 emphasized that the existence of a strike/lockout deadline in contract negotiations facilitates the process of reaching agreement because of the parties' mutual desire to avoid the consequences of failing to reach a timely settlement. A deadline provides a similar effect in bargaining the settlement of labor-management disputes in contract administration. The principal difference between the function of a deadline in contract negotiations and in contract administration is that in negotiations, the parties attempt to *decide on* their contractual obligations, while in administration, the potential consequence of failing to reach agreement serves to encourage both labor and management to *live up to* their contractual obligations.

A work stoppage in the form of strike or lockout is usually the only weapon that can be used directly by the negotiating parties to force agreement on a new contract. But in contract administration/dispute settlement, several other options are available to both labor and management. One option is the filing of lawsuits to recover damages resulting from contract violations. Another is the legal voiding of a contract which has been breached; and a third (available only to employers) is disciplinary action against workers who have violated the collective bargaining agreement. All of these options, however, may portend damage as serious to the labor-management relationship as the use of strike or lockout.

The vast majority of disputes arising during the life of a collective bargaining agreement are settled directly by the parties at some step of the grievance procedure. However, even under ideal circumstances, because of the basic adversary relationship between workers/union and employers, occasional disputes may arise where labor and management are unable to reach a mutually satisfactory agreement. The issue may be the correct interpretation of the contract, or it may be the appropriate manner for applying the terms of the contract. And where the labor relations environment is less than ideal, there may be fewer justifiable reasons for labor and management reaching the point of impasse—such as a worker/union move to flood the grievance procedure with numerous disputes in an effort to demonstrate strength and solidarity and thus win some specific concession from a frustrated management, or, on the other hand, an employer attempt to burden or embarrass the union by forcing it to bargain to the limit for each and every grievance settlement.

Regardless of the bargaining environment, both labor and management continually face the prospect of not reaching agreement as they consider the various stages of dispute settlement under contract administration. As a result of the likely possibility that they will reach the point of impasse sometime during the process of administering their contract, and as an alternative to using any of the various options involving force to back up their bargaining position, labor and management have increasingly turned to the practice of *arbitration* as a voluntary and peaceful last-resort means of settling intracontract differences. The mutual agreement, by contract, to submit such differences to a neutral third party for a final and binding decision has become one of the hallmarks of the American labor relations system.

In the early 1930s, about 10 percent of all collective bargaining agreements contained provisions for arbitration in the event of impasse over contract-administration disputes. By the mid-1940s, this figure had risen to about 75 percent; by the 1970s, it was over 95 percent. This growth in the use of arbitration is a result of the increasing status given arbitration by the Supreme Court (in the *Lincoln Mills* decision of 1957 and the Trilogy cases in 1960)[2] and by the NLRB in a 1971 decision which has come to be known as the *Collyer* doctrine.

Lincoln Mills articulated the principle that the agreement to arbitrate grievance disputes is the quid pro quo for an agreement not to strike during the life of a contract. The Trilogy cases reemphasized that arbitration is the preferred public policy for promoting peaceful settlement of labor-management disputes and limited the courts to a minor role in contract enforcement. In the Trilogy cases, the Supreme Court decreed the broad obligation of both labor and management to use arbitration, once agreed upon, stating that all matters covered by a collective bargaining agreement are potentially subject to arbitration. The Court also upheld the enforceability of arbitration awards, thus emphasizing its reluctance to substitute public policy for private contractual agreements in the resolution of labor relations disputes.

In 1971, in a split decision involving unfair labor practice charges, the National Labor Relations Board ruled that it would normally refuse to hear such cases if it was likely that the dispute could be settled through the arbitration clause of the parties' collective bargaining agreement. The essence of this ruling, which has subsequently been upheld in the federal courts, is that the NLRB—like the courts—is reluctant to take an active role in the settlement of labor relations disputes. Critics of the *Collyer* doctrine, however, claim that the Board has withdrawn too far and has thus jeopardized the statutory rights of those subject to unfair labor practices (especially workers and unions).

Principles and Procedures of Arbitration

The procedures of arbitration are characteristically similar throughout the tens of thousands of collective bargaining agree-

[2]The Trilogy cases were *Steelworkers v. American Manufacturing Co.*, *Steelworkers v. Warrior & Gulf Navigation Co.*, and *Steelworkers v. Enterprise Wheel & Car Corp.*

ments which call for this method of breaking impasse under contract administration. Likewise, certain principles of grievance arbitration are embodied in virtually all arbitration procedures.

The principle of voluntary, private arbitration of contract-administration disputes as an alternative to the use of force has evolved to the point of legal status. In *Teamsters v. Lucas Flour* (1962), the Supreme Court ruled that a contract's arbitration clause implies a joint labor-management pledge of no strikes or lockouts for the duration of the agreement. Thus, employers and unions can be held liable for damages resulting from strikes or lockouts in connection with disputes subject to the grievance procedure, regardless of whether their contracts contain an express no-strike clause. Furthermore, employers have the right to discipline and discharge workers who participate in such unlawful strikes (subject, of course, to appeal through the grievance procedure).

The final and binding nature of arbitration is also basic. The courts have repeatedly ruled that once labor and management agree to arbitrate contract-administration disputes they themselves cannot resolve, they are mutually bound to abide by the decision rendered. Thus the courts have routinely upheld the enforceability of arbitration awards so long as they do not expressly violate the terms and conditions of the contracts under which they are rendered.

A third principle fundamental to the concept of arbitration is the desirability of the parties' direct resolution of contract-administration disputes. Obviously, both unions and employers prefer to avoid the intervention of outsiders in the labor-management relationship. Accordingly, the knowledge that unless a settlement is reached internally the parties must cease bargaining and resort to outside resources encourages both labor and management to consider their respective positions very carefully.

Arbitration can be viewed as a judicial process; in effect, it is the court of last resort for contract-administration disputes. It is a serious undertaking which entails considerable responsibility for both labor and management. Of course, the arbitrator is the center of focus. Arbitration decisions not only are legally enforceable but also set precedents which may affect the course of future contract negotiations and administration.

The arbitration process usually includes a hearing where the disputants present and argue their respective positions. Although such hearings are generally conducted on a less formal basis than actual court proceedings, they often involve courtroom conventions such as the presentation of briefs, the use of exhibits and other forms of documentation, and the calling and cross-examination of witnesses.

The role of the arbitrator is to decide what *is,* not what ought to be. Decisions must be based on the language of the parties' contractual agreement. The fact that a particular portion of a collective bargaining agreement may be obviously unfair is irrelevant. The arbitration award must be based only on facts, arguments, and contract language. The arbitrator has no authority to change the content of the collective bargaining agreement, because to do so would undermine the very process of bilateral decision making that arbitration is designed to support.

If the contract provisions and facts in evidence are unmistakably clear and concise, the arbitrator will have little difficulty making a decision. The award will sustain the party whose position is supported by the facts and precise contract language. However, the majority of grievances that are arbitrated do not involve such clear issues, because cases which are so easily defined are usually settled through the grievance procedure. Arbitration most often decides issues of differing contract interpretation which labor and management have been unable to resolve to their mutual satisfaction. In such cases, where there is no precise and applicable contract language, the arbitrator is bound to use the *past practice* of the parties' experience with the collective bargaining agreement as the basis for making a determination. "Past practice" means the way labor and management have previously dealt with a problem or applied the terms of the contract. It can clarify ambiguous issues and language and can guide an arbitrator to a logical and contractually consistent award. But past practice is applicable only when there is an absence of precise contract language. The contract always takes precedence over practice. For example, even though an employer might deviate from the precise language of a contract for a considerable period of time (say, by paying workers every two weeks for two years of a three-year agreement which specifies that wages shall be paid weekly), past practice cannot be used as the basis for denying a union grievance demanding weekly paychecks.

Since an Arbitration award can be based only on factual evidence and supporting arguments, the need for thorough preparation by both parties should be obvious. Especially for the union, which is typically challenging some action or inaction on the part of the employer, the accumulation of all of the information relevant to a grievance and the organization of that evidence in a precise and logical manner are very important.

The arbitration award is a written document in which the arbitrator spells out the basic issues of the grievance, the relevant portions of the contract, and the position and arguments of both sides. The decision itself, either sustaining or denying the grievance and implying how the contract should be interpreted in the future, is routinely accompanied by an explanation of the rationale for the arbitrator's decision. In addition, special attention is usually given to explaining why the "losing" party's argument was denied.

Grievance arbitration is not part of the collective bargaining process in contract administration; arbitration is used when grievance bargaining breaks down and an impasse is reached. Accordingly, there is no room for counterproposals or any other form of give and take in arbitration. The opportunity to apply such strategies and techniques is during the process of bargaining at various steps of the grievance procedure. Thus, although the practice is widely frowned upon, there may be occasions, for example, when a union can trade the settlement of one grievance for the dropping of another, and still fulfill its obligation of fair and equal representation.

Once a grievance has been submitted to arbitration, the arbitrator must proceed on the assumption that the parties have already negotiated to the limit of their bargaining abilities and resources. Therefore the arbitrator must avoid the temptation to please both sides, either by effecting a compromise or, in a situation involving more than one grievance, by "splitting the difference"—deciding one case in favor of management and another in favor of the union. Each grievance arbitration must be decided individually. Obviously, the arbitrator has been called upon because the parties have been unable to reach agreement by themselves; the time for bargaining or even mediation to facilitate it has passed.

The arbitrator's award decides for the parties what they were incapable of deciding themselves. Once bargaining is over, the only choice is to decide fully in favor of one party or the other. If the evidence shows clearly that both parties are partially at fault, the arbitrator may in good conscience divide an award, but such a split decision should be clearly distinguishable from any attempt at compromise or appeasement.

Contract Provisions for Grievance Arbitration

While the general principles of arbitration are embodied in virtually every collective bargaining agreement that provides for its use in contract-administration disputes, detailed provisions for its implementation vary from agreement to agreement. One aspect which may vary is the scope of the grievance procedure, that is, exactly what issues are subject to bargaining and arbitration. Under most contracts, the issues to be grieved and those to be arbitrated are identical and include all matters covered by the agreement. However, contract-administration and dispute-settlement provisions are *mandatory* topics for negotiation; therefore, labor and management typically bargain over exactly which issues will be subject to the grievance procedure. Most contracts define grievances narrowly—for example, as disputes over the meaning and application of the contract language. A small proportion, however, define grievances quite broadly, to include any problem concerning wages, hours, working conditions, or other terms of employment.

In addition, labor and management may bargain over the exact provisions for the use of arbitration. Broad, inclusive language, for example, may stipulate that any grievance not settled directly by the parties will be submitted to arbitration within 30 days of the final grievance-step decision. Most exclusions from arbitration involve issues concerned with wage and effort scales, which both labor and management usually consider too fundamental to the collective bargaining relationship to be subject to outside determination. The contract language relating to such an exclusion might stipulate that disputes over wage rates, other economic benefits, and production standards are not subject to arbitration and that the parties' mutual no-strike/no-lockout agreement does not apply in resolving such disputes.

It is clear that the terminal point of the grievance procedure can be either arbitration or resort to the use of economic force. In the overwhelming majority of contracts, the terminal point is exclusively arbitration; in a smaller number, it is exclusively economic force; in the remainder, the specific issue determines the terminal point.

Who may file a grievance may also vary from contract to contract. Virtually all collective bargaining agreements allow individual workers or groups of workers to file grievances. In situations not specifically involving the union, however, many contracts prohibit the union itself from initiating grievances on behalf of workers. This type of contract language is particularly common in private industry, where Taft-Hartley amendments to the National Labor Relations Act permit individual workers to grieve without union representation as long as any settlement does not violate the collective bargaining agreement and the union is given an opportunity to be present at any settlement. As a way of encouraging workers to grieve on their own, therefore, many employers have insisted that the contract require grievances to be filed by individual workers or groups of workers, either with or without union representation. Unless a union expressly bargains away its right to file grievances, however, it retains the power to initiate them on behalf of its members.

Contracts also vary in the method by which arbitrators are selected and how they are to serve. Arbitrators may be selected by mutual agreement from a panel submitted by the American Arbitration Association or the Federal Mediation and Conciliation Service, by labor and management alternatively striking names from such a list, or by request to some designated agency or organization. The method of selection is usually related to the type of arbitration. If one arbitrator is to hear a single case, the contractual provisions for selection will probably be different from those for selecting a tripartite arbitration board (one person chosen by labor, another by management, and a neutral chair by agreement of the first two) or an individual or tripartite permanent arbitrator (whom the parties agree in advance will hear all grievance arbitrations).

The goal of labor and management in all of the various organizational arrangements for arbitration is to facilitate the timely resolution of contract-administration disputes and to provide for consistency in the interpretation and application of contract language. A trend in recent years has been toward permanent arbitrators, especially in large industries with multiemployer or multiunion contracts. Another recent innovation has been the negotiation of expedited arbitration proceedings to reduce the time between submission and the arbitration award. Numerous contracts today have both provisions.

A final area where contracts vary in regard to arbitration is the division of costs. Under most contracts, the arbitrator's fee is divided equally between the company and the union. Occasionally, though, a contract will call for one or the other party to bear a greater portion of the costs. Some contracts stipulate that each party will pay its own expenses for legal fees, transcripts, and lost time for witnesses. Others divide such expenses equally; still others require that management pay lost time to workers who appear at arbitration hearings and that all remaining incidental expenses be divided equally. A single arbitration case may cost thousands of dollars. Therefore, both labor and management have an interest in the exact provisions for handling such sizable expenses. How arbitration costs will be shared, like other matters relating to the establishment and function of dispute settlement procedures, is a mandatory bargaining topic.

Comparison of Craft and Industrial Union Contract Administration

The general principles of contract administration/dispute settlement are virtually identical in both craft and industrial union contracts, but detailed provisions for implementing these principles usually differ.

Regarding the *scope* of the grievance procedure, the tendency in craft union agreements is toward broad, inclusive definitions of the subject matter for contract administration. This broad definition acknowledges the craft union's important role in the employment relationship as well as the relatively high status and independence of the skilled craft worker. Many construction contracts, for example, simply state that any dispute arising on the job will be handled through the grievance machinery. In contrast, most industrial union contracts define grievances more narrowly. The employment relationship is generally more structured and authoritarian in industrial settings, so that management is in a better position to limit the overall participation of workers and their unions in the process of contract administration. This does not mean, however, that industrial unions are necessarily weaker than craft unions in their dealings with employers; it simply reflects different priorities. For example, most craft agreements are virtually silent with respect to discipline and discharge, while most industrial contracts contain specific language (often different and more stringent from that for handling all other grievances) for handling such disputes. The craft agreement, because of basic differences in the context of union, individual, and job security, does not need to carefully address the issues of discipline and discharge. The industrial contract, reflecting the nature of noncraft employment, does. As a result, many industrial workers enjoy very clearly defined protections against the arbitrary use of discipline and discharge by management.

A second distinction between craft and industrial union contract administration involves the *nature* of the grievance procedure and how union representatives participate in it. Craft agreements typically specify a two-step grievance procedure (including arbitration). As noted in Chapter 5, the steward on most craft jobs is simply a representative of the union's business agent. Therefore, in most craft agreements, if a dispute arises at the workplace, the steward is required to notify the business agent, who will negotiate directly with the employer. If the business agent and the employer cannot reach agreement, there is generally no higher level of union or management authority to appeal to, and impasse results. The usual exception to such a two-step grievance procedure is in association agreements between one or more craft unions and one or more employers, where it may be possible for representatives of the international union(s) and the association to continue bargaining at a higher level.

Industrial union grievance procedures are typically more hierarchical. Under most industrial union contracts, the steward is recognized as a union representative because, unlike a craft union steward who is appointed for a particular job with a given employer, the industrial union steward is in a position to maintain a continuous relationship with management. Thus the industrial union steward can be compared to the craft union business agent in a grievance procedure. Also in contrast to craft job stewards, industrial union stewards are typically chosen by the workers they represent and, like business agents, are the union's principal communication link with its membership.

The typical industrial union grievance procedure involves more than two steps. Most common is a three-step procedure (including arbitration) for individual grievances. The first step involves the steward and grieving worker(s) and the immediate supervisor; if the grievance remains unsettled, second-step negotiations include the local union grievance committee (often senior stewards and other local union officers) and plant management (usually the head of personnel or labor relations). A four-step grievance procedure is also common; prior to arbitration, negotiations are continued between local and international union officers and additional or other management officials. The four-step procedure is often negotiated in industries where a firm has numerous operations and thus "top" management at both the plant and corporate levels. Other grievance procedures may include five, six, or even more steps.

As mentioned in Chapter 4, assistance in the resolution of contract-administration disputes is one of the principal services provided by international unions to their local affiliates. This is especially the case among industrial unions, whose bargaining structures are more suited to such assistance than those of craft unions.

A third major difference between contract administration/dispute resolution in craft and industrial unions involves the *extent* to which arbitration is used in grievance settlement. Craft unions have traditionally used arbitration very sparingly, partly because of the lack of long-term union-employer relationships and partly because the strike has been a strategically more effective and manageable form of bargaining technique at craft job sites. Craft unions have increasingly been incorporating arbitration procedures into their contracts, however, especially where there is association bargaining. In some craft agreements, unsettled disputes are referred to a "board of adjustment" composed of equal numbers of union and employer representatives plus a neutral third or fifth member, whose majority opinion is binding on both parties. Such procedures are not usually specifically termed "arbitration," but they are unquestionably arbitration practices.

The use of arbitration by industrial unions has been widespread for many years, largely because of their emphasis on individual and job security and the desire by both unions and employers to settle disputes without interrupting production.

Special note should be made of the limited use of grievance arbitration in the public sector. As a rule (the usual exceptions being at the local government level in police and firefighter contracts), public sector collective bargaining agreements provide for arbitration of contract-administration disputes less often than private sector agreements. Lawmakers and civil service administrators in particular claim that such final and binding third-party decisions would undermine the ultimate, sovereign authority of government. As a result, most public sector unions are restricted to mediation and other nonbinding methods to assist in impasse resolution. As government-employee bargaining becomes more widespread, however, the present trend toward increasing acceptance of negotiated arbitration procedures is likely to continue, as it has in the private sector. At the same time, considerable effort is being devoted to developing workable alternatives to arbitration that can meet the special needs of both labor and management in the public sector.

A final distinction can be made in the way that different contract-administration procedures reflect the different organizational character of craft and industrial unions. For example, craft unions tend to be more centralized than industrial unions, especially at the local level, because of the nature of their markets, workplace technology, and accompanying power and influence relationships. Craft unions, therefore, seldom have multilevel systems of grievance representation, because such arrangements are impractical given the nature of the industries they deal with. Thus, while a two-step grievance procedure may appear to concentrate disproportionate power in the hands of the business agent, in actuality such an arrangement is merely a reflection of the craft environment.

Regardless of environment and specific procedures, the day-to-day administration of collective bargaining agreements, whether craft or industrial, has the significant effect of taking what was originally a static document and turning it into a dynamic instrument governing the complex and changing employment relationship. As responsible unions and employers apply the content of their negotiated contracts and settle disputes arising from them, it is almost inevitable that their relationship will mature. Contract administration through the negotiated settlement of grievances can thus be considered a cornerstone of labor-management relations—an inseparable part of the collective bargaining process.

Key Words and Phrases

American Arbitration Association
arbitration as a judicial process
association bargaining
board of adjustment
contract administration
duty to bargain
duty to furnish information in collective bargaining
express no-strike clause
expedited arbitration
final and binding arbitration
good-faith bargaining
grievance arbitration
grievance committee
grievance procedure
implied no-strike clause
"just cause"
"past practice"
permanent arbitrator
per se violations of the duty to bargain
scope of the grievance procedure
steps in a grievance procedure
terminal point in the grievance procedure
time limits in a grievance procedure
totality of conduct
the Trilogy cases
tripartite arbitration board
union steward

Review and Discussion Questions

1. Explain the logic of Justice Douglas' statement at the very beginning of this chapter.

2. Describe and explain the basic principles of grievance resolution as they apply to the contract administration/dispute settlement process.

3. Explain the importance of union representation in the process of labor-management communication and decision making, especially in the negotiation of grievance settlements.

4. Discuss the importance of good-faith bargaining and the duty to furnish information, particularly as they relate to contract administration.

5. Briefly describe the legal status of arbitration in the American labor relations system.

6. Why is preparation for arbitration so important for both labor and management?

7. What is the logic behind the assertion that, strictly speaking, arbitration is not part of the collective bargaining process? Do you agree or disagree?

8. What are the advantages of having arbitration as the terminal point in the grievance negotiation process? Are there any disadvantages? Are there alternatives to the arbitration of contract administration disputes?

9. Describe the basic functions and responsibilities of an arbitrator. What is the legal status of an arbitration award?

10. Construct diagrams illustrating typical two-, three-, and four-step grievance procedures (including arbitration). Be sure to indicate who is involved at each step to represent labor and management. Can you diagram a logical five-, six-, or seven-step grievance procedure using the same principles as for those with fewer steps?

11. Explain the basic differences between craft and industrial union organization for contract administration/dispute settlement.

12. The excessive use of arbitration may be a sign of immaturity in the collective bargaining relationship. Explain. What other reasons might be given for "too much" arbitration?

Chapter Resources and Suggested Further Reading

Complete bibliographical information for the following titles can be found in the Bibliography.

Repas, *Contract Administration: A Guide for Stewards and Local Officers.*

Richardson, *Collective Bargaining by Objectives.*

Sloane and Witney, *Labor Relations.*

Contract administration and dispute settlement:

Beal, Wickersham, and Kienast, "Agreement Administration," in *The Practice of Collective Bargaining.* (A comparison of craft and industrial union contract administration/dispute settlement procedures.)

BNA Editorial Staff, *Grievance Guide.* (A excellent reference on the subject of contract administration.)

Elkouri and Elkouri, *How Arbitration Works,* 4th Ed. (A comprehensive reference on the legal and procedural aspects of arbitration. Useful to both students and professionals, especially in its discussion of the various contract issues that are frequently arbitrated.)

Kuhn, James W., "The Grievance Process," in *Frontiers of Collective Bargaining,* by Dunlop and Chamberlain. (Discusses collective bargaining techniques and problems of grievance handling.)

Most large international unions publish their own stewards' manuals (similar to AFL-CIO publications for stewards); these manuals usually may be obtained at no charge.

But most important of all . . . for eighteen years I work in the Kelsey-Hayes foundry before the union, and for eighteen years they called me dumb Polack. And then the Union came along, and they call me brother.

—A retired auto worker, circa 1960

The steward's most important job is to see that grievances are settled. If you are a new steward, this may look like a tough job to you. Actually, it doesn't take the mind of a legal wizard—a little common sense and the courage to stand up for what's right will do the trick.

—From an International Molders and
Allied Workers Union *Steward's Manual*

The facts do not tell their own story: they must be cross-examined. They must be carefully analyzed, systematized, compared, and interpreted.

—Talcott Parsons, 1937

7

Issues, Prospects, and Perspectives*

> *They've been trying to tell us there are three separate groups . . . the company, the employees, and the union. . . . We have to show them they're wrong. . . . We have to show them there are not three groups but just two: the company and the union. Them and us.*
>
> —A local union officer during the GE strike (1969)

The preceding chapters have summarized the form and content of the American labor relations system. The descriptions of collective bargaining as the foundation of this system have emphasized historical, legal, functional, and structural aspects of the American labor movement. Through their unions, American workers have made considerable gains over the past 200 years, but thoughtful observation reveals a number of obstacles that remain to be overcome. Chapter 4 outlined some of the structural and administrative problems still facing American unions—in particular, education and communication, finance and administration, internal democracy and leadership development, and political activities. This chapter describes issues that are broader in scope and concludes with a statement of the prospects for labor relations in the twenty-first century.

*This chapter is based largely on the writings of Edwards, Reich, and Weisskopf; Kassalow; and Marshall, Briggs, and King. See Chapter Resources and Bibliography for specific references.

Technological Change, Business Organization, and Income Distribution

Since its inception, the labor movement has been on the defensive, attempting to prevent employers from exercising dictatorial powers over workers. For most of their 200-year history, American unions have fought simply for the right to be recognized and to have employers negotiate with them over the terms and conditions of employment. Recognition and bargaining rights, however, have not given workers a full voice in many basic economic decisions which ultimately affect them. An important example of this powerlessness is in the area of technological change.

Workers and unions have at best only limited control over the introduction of new technology which will affect their employment opportunities. American unions are thus compelled to accept unemployment as an inevitable result of labor-saving technology. Historically, the labor movement has had to fight a "rear guard" action, attempting to soften the harsh consequences of technological change through legislation or collective bargaining. Because they lack the statutory right to fully challenge management decisions to eliminate jobs through the introduction of more capital-intensive production processes, unions have had to work for better unemployment compensation measures when, under a different legal framework, they might well have been able to question whether—with virtually unlimited economic needs and wants—there should even *be* any unemployment.

Instances where unions have successfully resisted the introduction of labor-saving technologies are confined primarily to the skilled trades; but even in these occupations, the long-range trend is toward fewer new jobs, as management ultimately finds ways to substitute machine or manufacturing technologies for those of handicraft production.

Consequently, it can be said fairly that while the American labor movement has succeeded in protecting workers from actual starvation because of unemployment, it has been unable to guarantee that workers will have the opportunity to make an economic contribution instead of becoming an economic liability. Bluntly stated, the labor movement has not been in a position where it could effectively challenge the assertion that there is not enough work for everyone and that workers must therefore accept a certain amount of involuntary unemployment.

The twentieth century second industrial revolution based upon computers, robotics, and telecommunications portends economic, social, and even political change on an unprecedented scale. In short, space-age technology has given employers the means by which to radically alter the nature and content of work in the office as well as in the factory. And it has given others, like governments, a vehicle for fundamentally changing our social and political institutions. But as in the past, employers and politicians can expect union responses in proportion to the extent that workers are threatened or actually hurt by new technology.

The experts disagree on where the fast lanes of high-tech change will ultimately lead us. Some predict nirvana while others see only chaos on the horizon. Although the future likely will fall somewhere between these extremes, certain consequences of the computer age are highly predictable for workers and unions. For example, it is debatable whether this new technology in the long run will create more jobs than it eliminates. But unquestionably, the skill requirements as well as the organization of work in the office and factory of the future will be much different than in the past.

For the labor movement, the most important issues in terms of organizing and representation will be related to the rate of change, as distinct from change itself. As in the past, workers and unions continue to have little if any control over the nature of technological change. However, the environment within which such change takes place is, at least potentially, within the domain of worker/union control—especially where collective bargaining exists.

By confronting the basically unplanned nature of technological change under market capitalism, the labor movement can lessen the impact on those most vulnerable to its consequences. Particularly threatened are assembly and clerical jobs involving manual as opposed to cognitive skills—occupations traditionally concentrated among the young, the old, women, and migrant workers.

Nationally, the goal should be to produce a labor force whose skill mix of education and vocational training keeps pace with the nature of technological change. At the community and workplace levels, the labor movement can work to see that both the costs and benefits of economic progress are shared equitably by workers and employers. By taking these steps, unions can directly counter the tendency for businesses to externalize the costs of technological change—namely upon individual workers, communities, and the larger society.

Closely related to the issue of technological change is the question of business organization. In the 1960s and 1970s, the pace of conglomerate and multinational expansion accelerated dramatically. Thousands of international corporate operations have been established, including some country-company multinationals, formed by corporations and the governments of countries with centrally planned economies.

The single most compelling reason for the expansion of multinational business activities has been the quest for profits. Hundreds of thousands of American manufacturing jobs have been "exported" in recent years to countries where labor can be obtained more cheaply and where production can be closer to foreign markets, with fewer constraints on labor relations, occupational safety and health, and environmental protection.

American unions have succeeded in establishing legal protections and economic benefits superior to those for workers in less developed economies. However, they have failed to achieve effective mechanisms for preventing employers from escaping their obligations in one country by moving to another.

In simple terms, the domestic problem of the "runaway" shop (firms or plants moving from the organized northern and midwestern states to the South and West where it is more difficult for workers to organize) has become international in nature and consequence.

Through its trade secretariats, the international labor movement has recently increased its efforts to deal with multinational business issues which affect workers. The World Auto Councils, a part of the International Metalworkers Federation, has developed the most extensive programs to date. The unions of virtually all of the world's major automobile producers share information about their respective companies, and when problems arise for one of the Councils' members, the others coordinate their support in whatever ways seem most appropriate. However, the auto unions are essentially confined to defensive measures, such as official protests and financial support of weaker members. Unable to change the fundamental nature of business organization, the unions have been forced to deal with the consequences of their relative powerlessness rather than its causes.

A third area of economic decision making where the labor movement is relatively powerless involves the distribution of income, that is, the share of the rewards of their production that workers receive in the form of wages. While unions have substantially increased the real wages of workers, economic statistics indicate that between 1950 and 1975 very little change occurred in the distribution of income in the United States between workers and employers. Labor's absolute share of national income remained about 70 to 75 percent.

The relative proportions of wages received by union and nonunion workers, however, have changed over the years, especially in industries that are heavily organized or that have particularly strong unions. Most studies of such industries show, however, that wage levels achieved through collective bargaining are seldom more than 25 percent higher than those in similar nonunion enterprises. The question is further complicated by the nonmonetary benefits which derive from union activity. Union leaders as well as rank-and-file members are correct in emphasizing the intangible benefits of union organization; to be treated with dignity, respect, and fairness on the job has no dollar value, but it nonetheless represents a significant achievement for workers. However, the labor movement understandably has been reluctant to confront the implications of a rising relative wage share for organized workers, in light of the essentially constant absolute share for all workers as a whole. The economic gains of union members have apparently been achieved less at the expense of employers as a whole than at the expense of nonunion workers. Employers have evidently been able to compensate for improvements in wages and working conditions for union members by increasing their exploitation of unorganized workers, despite the positive influence of union wage scales on those of nonunion employers.

In addition, unions are limited in their power to increase their share of business proceeds over the long run. For example, while they may be able to negotiate higher wages and thus temporarily increase the economic welfare of their members relative to the employer, unions have no control over what businesses charge for their products or services, and employers, therefore, have the last word. Likewise, the costs of wage increases and other benefits may be reduced through the introduction of new technology or the transfer of work to lower-wage facilities in other states or countries.

In contrast to the widespread prosperity of the 1950s and 1960s, current indications are that the United States is moving toward a two-tier society where the rich are growing richer at the expense of a shrinking middle class and growing outright poverty. Between 1970 and 1985, the portion of family heads earning less than enough to sustain a family of four at the poverty level rose from around one in five to nearly one in three. The majority of this increase came from families "slipping" into poverty because of falling wages relative to higher living costs.

The fact that union representation (with accompanying higher wages) fell during this time is one explanation of the trend toward greater income inequality. But the wage and benefit concessions extracted from organized workers in the late seventies and eighties also lowered the living standard of many if not most union members. What remains to be seen is whether the labor movement can prevent further economic losses for the organized and thus set an example for the unorganized. If this *can* be done, the potential for a resurgence in union growth would be enhanced considerably.

Ultimately, reversing the trend toward a two-tier society will involve political as well as collective bargaining solutions. This is yet another reason for workers to see unions as the way out of their current predicament. However, if the labor movement is to lead the way in preventing workers from being hurt by technological change and its effects on business organization and income distribution, its agenda and actions must be carried out in the political arena as well as at the bargaining table.

Sexual and Racial Discrimination

As suggested above, many of the problems facing American workers and unions in the late twentieth century appear to be systemic in nature and thus not easily resolved within the framework of collective bargaining. Sexual and racial discrimination, for example, has persisted and in some respects has increased in spite of widespread union organization. True, legislation such as the Equal Pay Act of 1963 and the Civil Rights Act of 1964 has improved the legal status of women and minorities in the labor force, but employment and income statistics reveal little real progress where it counts most—on the economic front.

Between 1900 and 1985, the labor force participation of women tripled, from around 20 percent to over 60 percent of all women of working age. During the same period, women as a percentage of the labor force increased from slightly over 18 percent to nearly 45 percent. However, increases in the number and percentage of women working outside the home have not been accompanied by improvements in their economic status relative to male workers. Between 1955 and 1980, the median income of fulltime women workers as a percentage of that for full-time male workers actually decreased from about 64 percent to about 59 percent.

Part of the reason women workers on the average earn much less than male workers is because women have historically been concentrated in lower paying jobs, such as secretarial work, retail sales, bookkeeping, and waitressing. Even in higher paying professional and technical occupations, the incomes earned by women are only about two thirds of those earned by men.

The reasons for continuing economic discrimination against women are varied and complex, but underlying them all is the history of social organization in the United States. While the United States was primarily an agricultural economy, families supported themselves as an economic unit. There was essentially no distinction between raising food, weaving cloth, caring for children, and maintaining a household. Because most families were self-sufficient, the division of labor for these tasks was relatively unimportant, because all of the tasks were necessary to maintain the household and because there was little need for outside income.

With the advent of industrialization and the wage labor system, however, someone had to leave the home to provide money for the family. Because women alone were capable of bearing children, it seemed most logical for women to remain at home and assume the task of raising them and maintaining the household. Thus industrialization created an artificial distinction between work for which wages were paid and work which maintained a family and household but which did not produce actual money income.

In a society where social and political power depends on personal wealth, income, and occupation, it is not surprising that women, whose economic contribution has not been traditionally recognized, are generally regarded as a less valuable work force than men. Although both men and women workers today have similar education, women are still excluded from numerous occupations. This exclusion forces many women to take jobs for which they are overqualified, thus depressing wages in such occupations because of the abundance of available workers.

At one time, it could have been argued that most women did not need to work; only some widows and unmarried women without family were forced to seek employment to support themselves. At present, however, nearly 10 million American families are headed by women—who are, therefore, the principal source of economic support for such households. In addition, many American families would be unable to survive without the incomes of both husband and wife; for many women, to work has become an economic necessity.

While women workers have long been an important and growing element of the total labor force, their involvement in labor or-

Bricklayers union in Jacksonville, Fla., circa 1900.

Pennsylvania Historical Collections, Pattee Library, Pennsylvania State University

Women workers in the trim department of the John B. Stetson (Hat) Company, circa 1915.

Archives of Labor and Urban Affairs, Wayne State University

ganizations has increased even more rapidly, especially in recent years. By 1985, six million women were union members. They represented nearly a third of the organized labor movement and earned wages 30 percent higher than their nonunion counterparts, regardless of industry.

Within the American labor movement, the Coalition of Labor Union Women (CLUW) was formed in 1974 to develop action programs to bring more of the nation's 35 million women workers into unions and to increase the leadership abilities of the 4.5 million women who are union members. CLUW has sponsored legislative proposals to improve job safety and health standards, to establish child care facilities, and to extend protective legislation for both men and women. With the backing of national AFL-CIO resolutions, CLUW campaigned for the Equal Rights Amendment to the Constitution, reasoning that women will be unable to achieve full legal, political, and social equality until they have an explicit constitutional guarantee of equal citizenship rights with men.

While affirmative action programs have had some success in increasing the number of women in predominately male, higher-paying occupations, there has been little progress in reducing overall male/female wage disparities. This is because most women are still confined to lower-paying "female occupations" involving secretarial, sales, and service work.

The newest approach of the labor movement to this problem, particularly among those sensitive to women's issues, has been to equalize the evaluation of women's and men's jobs. The charge is one of long-standing discrimination in the process of determining the worth of specific occupations. For example, parking lot attendants and zoo keepers (predominately males) typically earn more than nursery school teachers and day care workers (predominately females), despite the latter's greater training and responsibility.

The pay equity (or comparable worth) movement seeks wage levels that correspond more closely to the skill requirements as well as the value of the work being performed. Simply put, the argument is that jobs involving equal or comparable responsibility and education/training should be paid on an equal or comparable basis, regardless of whether they are held predominately by men or women.

As a result of union initiatives, numerous pay equity actions are currently pending in the nation's courts and legislatures. But with the economic stakes so high, it is unlikely that the issue will be resolved without considerable resistance on the part of employers in both the private and public sectors.

Similarly, despite the statutory elimination of barriers to full equality for black, Hispanics, and other racial minorities, economic statistics indicate that racism is still very much institutionalized in American society. Nonwhite workers, like women, have traditionally been confined to lower-skilled, lower-paying jobs. At the same time, technological advances have decreased employment opportunities by eliminating many jobs that require less education and training. The economic position of nonwhites has improved over the last two decades, but that improvement is only a relative one. Between 1955 and 1985, for example, the median income of nonwhite males increased from about 50 percent to nearly 70 percent of that for white males.

Although the labor movement has been criticized for its complicity in perpetuating racial discrimination, there is some evidence that racially restrictive policies of unions have been motivated primarily by economic considerations. In the construction crafts, for example, job security has been enhanced by restricting the supply of skilled craft workers. This restriction, combined with the tradition of passing the trade from father to son, encouraged craft unions to establish exclusionary practices (particularly regarding apprenticeship openings) or to condone segregated locals where there were large numbers of nonwhite craft workers.

Employers, however, have benefited the most from discriminatory practices. Employers may be able to keep wages low for white workers (especially men) if such workers are persuaded that they may be replaced by blacks (or women) if they demand higher pay. In addition, by encouraging workers to align themselves along racial lines against each other, employers can discourage worker unity and militance. Thus discrimination operates to the detriment of all workers.

Overall, the net impact of unions on the equal employment opportunities of both men and women and minorities has certainly been positive. At the national level, the labor movement, more than any other single institution, has consistently fought for civil rights, improved education, and other social and economic legislation of benefit to all workers regardless of age, color, sex, or union membership for that matter. At the local level, while there have been exceptions, unions as a whole (especially in the industrial and public sectors) have been in the forefront of the drive for job equality.

Economic discrimination against minority and women workers remains one of the most serious problems confronting the labor movement. In short, it will be difficult to achieve an acceptable standard of living for *all* workers so long as *some* workers are excluded from full equality.

Unions in Other Developed Economies

Our discussion so far has focused on labor relations in the United States. However, in order to better understand the approach of American unions to the employment relationship, we should examine how unions in other countries have dealt with similar issues.

The only other large geographic area with a long history of industrialization and union activity is western Europe.[1] The western European labor movement, like that of the United States, was founded in the last half of the nineteenth century. The economic forces responsible for the formation of both labor movements were basically the same—namely, the rapid growth of industrialization and wage labor under capitalism. But the social and political forces accompanying western European and American capitalism were sufficiently dissimilar to produce distinctly different types of union organization, with fundamentally different goals and objectives. Most important, while the American labor movement embraced *business unionism,* with its emphasis on immediate, job-related issues, the western European labor movement as a whole was more deeply influenced by Marxist and other socialist/anarchist doctrines of the time and thus originated with *revolutionary unions* seeking to replace private ownership of the means of production with worker-controlled institutions. Although their philosophical differences have narrowed over the years (largely as a result of western European unions becoming more business-union-like in their practices), the effects of markedly different origins are still clearly apparent.

One principal difference between the American and western European labor movements is the role taken by government in the realm of economic affairs, in particular regarding labor-management relations. In the United States, before 1935, government intervention in labor relations was directed primarily to the protection of property rights; employers were not required to heed the demands of workers for union organization. Thus the American labor movement was founded and grew within a framework of distrust for

[1]Countries included are Austria, Belgium, Denmark, England, Finland, France, Iceland, Ireland, Italy, Luxembourg, Netherlands, Norway, Portugal, Spain, Sweden, Switzerland, and West Germany.

government. Unions quite understandably wanted no more from government than the legal right to exist and to have employers compelled to negotiate with them over the terms and conditions of employment. In western Europe, however, greater class solidarity and political orientation led unions to seek many of their objectives through legislation. Accordingly, western European unions have continually sought government intervention, whereas American unions have traditionally demanded that government keep out of labor-management affairs. Such different approaches have had strikingly different consequences for the labor relations system.

In western Europe, the scope of bargaining is narrow compared to that in the United States, because many of the items subject to contract negotiation in the United States are regulated by law in western European countries. For example, supplemental benefits such as vacations and holidays, medical and dental coverage, and pension and retirement plans are legislated in most western European countries and are available to all workers, whether or not they are union members.[2]

Another area of sharp contrast between American and western European labor relations is the relative importance of union and individual/job security measures. Nowhere in western Europe, for example, is there a counterpart to the National Labor Relations Board, with its complex system of union certification and administrative law, because for the most part, western European employers have accepted the institutional role of unions. In addition, European unions have been able to rely on a greater sense of worker commitment to the labor movement and have thus found it unnecessary to acquire security through closed or union shop provisions or dues checkoff.[3]

Job security based on the use of seniority systems has been relatively uncommon with western European unions because of government limitations on the right of employers to lay off workers and the existence of comprehensive public policies to protect the unemployed through retraining and relocation allowances, income maintenance, and other assistance programs.

A third principal difference between American and European labor relations is in contract administration/dispute settlement pro-

[2]Increasingly, however, western European unions have considered such legislation as establishing a *minimum* and have negotiated additional benefits for their members, over and above those provided by government.

[3]Around 60 percent of European workers are union members, compared to less than 20 percent in the United States, which is the least organized industrial economy in the world.

cedures. The tradition in western Europe of providing statutory rather than collectively bargained protections for workers has natural implications for grievance adjudication. Arbitration is almost never used; instead, labor-management disputes are referred to government-operated "labor courts." These courts are part of the legal system and usually hear cases and enforce decisions in the same way as other courts.

Fourth, in most western European nations, there is no *single* labor federation corresponding to the AFL-CIO in the United States. Instead, the labor movement in these countries typically involves two or more major confederations. Belgium, Denmark, France, Italy, Holland, Spain, and Sweden all have multiple federations based upon capitalist, communist, or socialist political platforms. Britain and West Germany are the only large industrial economies with only one major labor federation.

All of these differences have had significant effects on the basic labor relations environments of Europe and the United States. The European labor movement is more nationally centralized because of its greater involvement in national politics and also because it deals with a more centralized industrial structure. At the same time, however, the narrower scope of bargaining at the job site has prompted western European workers and unions to seek direct involvement in the management of industry through various "codetermination" plans.

In Great Britain, for example, most larger enterprises have joint worker-management councils that communicate over a broad range of business decisions, including finance, production, personnel, and employee welfare. These councils, however, are officially independent of union influence and are only advisory. In West Germany, the concept of codetermination has been expanded to the point where in certain major industries, such as steel and coal, representatives of both workers and the union hold top management positions (among them membership on boards of directors) with their firms. Throughout western Europe, however, codetermination plans have elicited mixed reactions from the labor movement. Some workers and union officials feel that such labor participation can improve labor relations; others condemn it as an endorsement of capitalism which will eventually erode worker and union power.

As in the United States and western Europe, unions throughout the world are highly reflective of the overall social, political, and (especially) economic environments within which they exist. For all countries, the form of unionism tends not to remain fixed. Instead, unions develop and change in response to both internal and external influences on the nature and content of the employment experience. Some descriptions of this dynamic process can be instructive.

In Brazil, for example, gradual democratization beginning in the late 1970s prompted the reemergence of an independent and increasingly militant labor movement. Prior to 1977, four decades of military dictatorship and civil repression had all but eliminated unions as part of the economic and political process. But over the next few years, the influence of unions and collective bargaining in Brazilian society increased dramatically. By 1985, Brazilian unions had gained not only a strong voice in decisions at the workplace (especially in the industrial sector), but also were positioned to affect the country's political future. The case of Brazil is currently one where the future of the labor movement is highly dependent on continuing political, as well as economic, stability and progress.

The Canadian labor movement in recent years can be contrasted with its neighbor to the south. Significantly, both U.S. and Canadian workers (many of them represented by the same stateside international unions) have faced similar problems stemming from international trade and technological change. However, compared to quite similar responses in the 1940s, 1950s, and 1960s, the U.S. and Canadian labor movements of the 1970s and 1980s have evolved in different directions. The Canadian response to the current economic crisis has been for labor, management, and government to jointly search for solutions to their respective but related problems—to a much greater degree than has been so in the United States. In the United States, both corporate and public officials have shown little interest in making labor a full partner in the political economy. As a result of these developments, and compared to 20 years ago, the Canadian labor movement appears to be growing less like its United States counterpart while heading in the direction of the European experience.

Japanese unions also mirror the country's historical experience, especially in regard to social and political traditions. In fact, among the world's three economic superpowers, Japan is marked by the greatest contrasts; and so too is its labor movement.

Two predominant factors influencing the form of Japanese unions are the highly-segmented nature of the economy and the lower status of women in society. Economic segmentation, the existence of a relatively few giant, unionized industrial corporations at one extreme and thousands of small, nonunion "garage-shop" suppliers at the other, has tied most unions to individual employers.

The predominance of such "enterprise unions" has hampered the formation of a national, federated labor movement such as exists in the United States. The lower status of women, by definition, has fostered sharp divisions in the labor force, with harmful effects on the prospects for building broad worker/union solidarity. A cumulative result of such economic and social extremes is an employment system that currently provides lifetime job security to a few workers at the expense of most others.

Politically, while of late there has been broad and ideologically diversified input, the Japanese government has continued to exert great influence over the nation's economic decision-making process. Over time, however, a worker/union-led clash between the realities of twenty-first century technology and Japan's pre-industrial social mores seems inevitable. From this conflict will emerge a much different Japanese labor movement than exists today.

South Africa in the mid-1980s represents yet another distinct example of the origins and development of a national labor movement. The struggle to end apartheid's minority white rule took on new meaning when the government reluctantly legalized black labor unions in 1979.

Black South African workers joined unions in great numbers over the next several years and, as a result, became not only an economic force at the workplace but an organized political force as well. In 1985, the beginnings of a federated labor movement took shape with the formation of the Congress of South African Trade Unions (Cosatu) involving more than 30 separate unions. With a membership of over 500,000, Cosatu, along with other unaffiliated unions and smaller labor federations, now represents a base for labor activism in the larger society.

Yet problems including internal political divisions (on anti-apartheid strategies) and the fear of violent, government repression have made the future of a united black South African labor movement uncertain. In addition are sensitive questions concerning the eventual unification of black *and* white unions.

Perhaps nowhere else in the world today is there an emerging labor movement facing such challenges as well as the opportunity to shape history. Almost certainly, the future of South Africa, and likely that of much of the rest of the continent, will rest on the fate of its fledgling unions in the months and years ahead.

Despite their many differences, the unions and labor movements discussed above function basically within capitalist economies and therefore can be contrasted with unions in countries with socialist economies. In theory, the major difference in labor relations between capitalist and socialist countries is that under capitalism, there is direct competition between workers and employers for the proceeds of production, while under socialism, workers (through their government) own and control the enterprises that employ them. In practice, however, disputes between workers and managers are inevitable in both socialist and capitalist economies, and mechanisms must be developed for handling them.

Most recently, the Polish Solidarity movement has demonstrated the potential for conflict between labor and management in state-controlled economies. But in most socialist countries, unions are openly accepted and play a vital albeit different role than their counterparts under capitalism. Under socialism, since there is no private (profit-oriented) ownership of the basic means of production and since production and distribution usually are more centrally planned (rather than determined in the marketplace), the activities of unions are directed toward achieving national goals while protecting the interests of workers.

In the Soviet Union and East Germany for example, union organization is extensive but there is no "labor movement" as we know it in the West. In these countries, union representatives, elected by and accountable to the workers, serve on government committees responsible for determining production goals, wage levels, and other work-related activities. In addition, at the local level, unions typically negotiate collective bargaining agreements with the managers of the workplace; grievances are decided by local union-management committees—subject to court appeal—and it is not uncommon for managers to be removed because of complaints against them by the workers.

Workplace health and safety is an area where unions tend to be especially influential under socialism. In countries as diverse as Romania and Cuba, workers and union representatives have effective power over unsafe working conditions. In these and other socialist countries, occupational safety and health training for all workers is typically mandated by law and unions are empowered to monitor and force the correction of hazardous working conditions.

From this brief look at unions in other countries, at least one important conclusion can be drawn. While there is certainly room for debate over the fundamental differences in economic organization and policy from country to country, unions everywhere can learn from each other. In short, protecting the rights and interests of workers is a universal goal which transcends geographic boundaries and ideological differences.

Responding to the Challenges of an Uncertain Future

Of course, it is impossible to predict accurately the course of labor relations in the United States or in any other country. The history of labor movements, however, provides a basis for speculation on their continued progress. Unresolved issues of technological change, business organization, and income distribution, in addition to problems of economic discrimination and union administration, are likely to continue to be major challenges to the ability of American unions to effect meaningful changes in behalf of their members.

In general, unions in socialist countries and in western Europe have a greater say in basic economic decisions than unions in the United States, primarily because a much higher percentage of their workers are organized, and because there is greater government protection of the basic economic rights of all citizens—whether union members or not. Especially in light of a less protective legal environment, the relatively small proportion of American workers who are presently organized (officially less than 20 percent) remains a sizable obstacle to effective union participation in economic affairs. Compared to 1945, when close to 40 percent of American workers were union members, the power and influence of the American labor movement have actually declined over the last four decades—according to this measure, by nearly one half.

The problem of declining union power and influence is circular in nature and consequences. Declines in membership weaken the labor movement, which makes it even more difficult to organize workers, who see less to be gained from union membership. Because of declining political power, the American labor movement has been unable to improve significantly the legal environment within which it must function. An unfavorable legal environment, in turn, has reduced the economic power of unions at the bargaining table. Internally, the overall lack of progress in solving problems of discrimination and their exclusion from decisions which address issues such as inflation and unemployment have led, paradoxically, to both apathy and revolt by many union members.

In 1965 noted author and historian Michael Harrington, speaking to the Midwest Labor Press Association at the University

Garment workers demonstrate their cultural solidarity at New York Labor Day parade, 1982.

UAW Solidarity Magazine/Dotter

Jobs and special justice rally in Philadelphia, 1983.

UAW Solidarity Magazine/West

of Iowa, reminded his audience that unions had done more to abolish poverty in America than any other institution. At the same time, however, he pointed out that in order to confront the challenges of the future successfully, unions would have to recapture the sense of solidarity and movement that characterized their past, especially the 1930s and 1940s, when labor was crusading for fundamental changes in American society.

The labor movement of the 1930s and 1940s prospered because it produced visible and meaningful results for American workers: the right to organize and bargain collectively with their employers. In the 1980s and beyond, workers and unions will need to devote comparable energy to resolving remaining problems if they are to rekindle the spirit and determination of the labor movement.

In fact, there are signs that such a resurgence is currently underway. In 1982, the AFL-CIO Executive Council established the Committee on the Evolution of Work to review and evaluate changes taking place in American society. In 1983, the committee issued an initial report, *The Future of Work,* which detailed economic and demographic changes affecting the growth and stability of the United States labor force. In 1985, a second report, *The Changing Situation of Workers and Their Unions,* prescribed a plan for adapting to the rapidly changing world of work by increasing the involvement of labor in decisions affecting our collective future.

The *Changing Situation of Workers and Their Unions* was an admission that unions had fallen "behind the pace of change." But even more important was the assertion that unions must "continue to play a civilizing, humanizing, and democratizing role in American life," as they have in the past.

While the problems facing the American labor movement are probably as great as in any previous historical period, there is ample proof of labor's ability to respond to adversity and convert temporary weakness into lasting strength. Yet perhaps as never before, such progress will be difficult to sustain, primarily because of the increasing pace of technological change. The challenge to labor will be that of adhering to basics (workplace democracy and community involvement) in the face of continually shifting political and economic priorities imposed by forces largely beyond their control.

In addition to structural questions of economic organization and policy, the labor movement must resolve internal issues related to the aspirations of workers confronting the dawn of the "information age." In 1984, Harvard University economists Freeman and

Medoff published their classic, "*What Do Unions Do,*" in which they documented the predominant benefits of unions in American society. Their conclusion, that the "collective voice-institutional response" role of unions which enables them to channel worker discontent into improved workplace conditions, lies at the heart of labor's future, both here and abroad.

More than a hundred years ago, in 1884, Eugene V. Debs, reflecting on the loss of the Pullman strike, said,

> Ten thousand times has the labor movement stumbled and bruised itself. We have been enjoined by the courts, assaulted by thugs, traduced by the press, frowned upon by public opinion, and deceived by politicians.
>
> But notwithstanding all this and all these, labor today is the most vital and potential power this planet has ever known, and its historic mission is as certain of ultimate realization as is the setting of the sun.

Thus, from Debs to Freeman and Medoff and beyond, it should be clear that what made unions a vital component of the struggle for economic and social justice in the past continues to make them central to the democratic process today. The ideals, as well as the practice, of economic and political democracy call for the inclusion of workers and their representative (union) organizations as full and equal partners in the quest for social progress.

Key Words and Phrases

absolute and relative wage shares
apartheid
apprenticeship
class solidarity
Coalition of Labor Union Women (CLUW)
codetermination plan
comparable worth
conglomerate
Congress of South African Trade Unions (COSATU)
country-company multinational
economic segmentation
enterprise union
Equal Rights Amendment (ERA)
income distribution
institutionalized racism
labor court
labor-saving technology
multinational business
pay equity
runaway shop
second industrial revolution
systemic problems
technological change
two-tier society
World Auto Councils

Those who currently celebrate the weakening of unions and anticipate their eventual demise should remember that similar predictions have only served to renew the labor movement. As the great philosopher Yogi Berra once said, "It just might be *deja vu* all over again."

Review and Discussion Questions

1. What reasons can you give for the continuing economic discrimination against women and minority workers in the United States, in spite of improved legal protections?
2. In what ways do union organization and collective bargaining tend to eliminate racial and sexual discrimination?
3. Given the fact that union wages have an upward effect on nonunion wages, how is it possible that employers can compensate for union gains by further exploiting the unorganized?
4. Do you agree with this chapter's assertion that workers and unions in the United States have been denied a voice in many of the basic economic decisions affecting them? Why or why not?
5. Is there any justification for unions rather than employers controlling the introduction of new technology in our economy? What would be the most likely management response to this question?
6. The only way workers can effectively deal with multinational corporations is through "multinational unions." Do you agree? Why or why not? What alternatives do workers and unions have?
7. Why have American unions been unsuccessful in changing the distribution of income between workers and employers? What would be needed to accomplish such a goal?
8. The labor movements of the United States and western European countries are distinctly different. What are the principal differences, and what caused these differences?
9. What are the distinguishing differences between labor relations systems in capitalist and socialist countries? Do you think these differences will tend to erode over time? Why or why not?
10. What lessons do you think can be learned by U.S. unions from those in other countries; and vice versa?
11. In light of the fundamental differences between capitalist and socialist economies, comment on the statement that disputes between workers and managers are common to all employment situations, and mechanisms must be developed for handling them.
12. What would be the likely effects on the American labor relations system if, instead of one fifth, four fifths of all workers belonged to unions?
13. What do *you* predict will be the state of U.S. labor-management relations in the year 2000?

Chapter Resources and Suggested Further Reading

Complete bibliographical information for the following titles can be found in the Bibliography.

Committee on the Evolution of Work, *The Changing Situation of Workers and Their Unions.*
Committee on the Evolution of Work, *The Future of Work.*
Edwards, Reich, and Weisskopf, *The Capitalist System.*
Juris, Thompson, and Daniels, Eds., *Industrial Relations in a Decade of Economic Change.*
Kassalow, *Trade Unions and Industrial Relations: An International Comparison.*
Marshall, Briggs, and King, *Labor Economics.*
Sturmthal, *Comparative Labor Movements.*

Contemporary labor problems and issues:

Beirne, *Challenge to Labor: New Roles for American Unions.*
Bluestone, Harrison, and Baker, *Corporate Flight.*
Bok and Dunlop, *Labor and the American Community.*
Kochan, *Challenges and Choices Facing American Labor.*
Kochan, Katz, and McKensie, *The Transformation of American Industrial Relations.*
Montgomery, *Worker Control in America.*
Wortman, *Critical Issues in Labor.*

Racial and sexual discrimination:

Andreas, *Sex and Caste in America.*
Jones, *Prejudice and Racism.*
Needleman, Ed., "Turning the Tide: Women, Unions, and Labor Education," Theme Issue, *Labor Studies Journal.*

Unions and multinationals:

Bluestone and Bennett, *The Deindustrialization of America.*
Hershfield, *The Multinational Union Challenges the Multinational Company.*

Economic discrimination and income distribution in the American economy:

Cohen, "Wage Analysis," in *Labor in the United States.*
Edwards, Reich, and Weisskopf, "The Functioning of Capitalism in America," in *The Capitalist System.*
Harrington, *The New American Poverty.*

Marshall, Cartter, and King, "Minority Employment and Income Problems" and "Labor Issues of the Future," in *Labor Economics.*

Rees, "The Influence of Unions on Relative Earnings," in *An Anthology of Labor Economics: Readings and Commentary* by Marshall and Perlman.

The problem in America is not that the top 100 corporation presidents are violating the laws, though God knows they are; the problem is they're writing the laws.

—Nicholas Johnson,
Federal Communications Commission, 1972

The United States is substantially challenged to demonstrate that it can abolish not only racism but the scourge of poverty of whites as well as Negroes and the horrors of war that transcend national borders and involve all mankind.

—Martin Luther King, 1968

Democracy cannot be static. Whatever is static is dead.

—Eleanor Roosevelt, circa 1940

The strongest bond of human sympathy, outside the family relation, should be one uniting all working people, of all nations, and tongues and kindreds.

—Abraham Lincoln, 1864

Bibliography

Anderson, Howard J. *Primer of Labor Relations.* 21st ed. Washington, D.C.: The Bureau of National Affairs, Inc., 1980.

Andreas, Carol. *Sex and Caste in America.* Englewood Cliffs, N.J.: Prentice-Hall, 1971.

Beal, Edwin F.; Wickersham, Edward D.; and Kienast, Philip. *The Practice of Collective Bargaining.* Homewood, Ill.: Richard D. Irwin, 1972.

Beirne, Joseph A. *Challenge to Labor: New Roles for American Unions.* Englewood Cliffs, N.J.: Prentice-Hall, 1969.

Bloom, Gordon, and Northrup, Herbert. *Economics of Labor Relations.* Homewood, Ill.: Richard D. Irwin, 1965.

Bluestone, Barry; Harrison, Bennett; and Baker, Lawrence. *Corporate Flight.* Washington, D.C.: Progressive Alliance, 1981.

BNA Editorial Staff. *Grievance Guide.* 6th ed. Washington, D.C.: The Bureau of National Affairs, Inc., 1982.

Bok, Derek C., and Dunlop, John T. *Labor and the American Community.* New York: Simon & Schuster, 1970.

Boyer, Richard, and Morais, Herbert. *Labor's Untold Story.* New York: United Electrical, Radio, & Machine Workers, 1977.

Brooks, Thomas R. *Toil and Trouble: A History of American Labor.* New York: Dell Publishing Co., Delta Books, 1972.

Butler, Arthur D. *Labor Economics and Institutions.* New York: Macmillan Co., 1963.

Cahn, William. *A Pictorial History of American Labor.* New York: Crown Publishers, 1972.

Cohen, Sanford. *Labor in the United States.* Columbus, Ohio: Charles E Merrill Publishing Co., Div. of Bell & Howell Co., 1975.

Caute, David. *The Great Fear: the Anti-Communist Purge Under Truman and Eisenhower.* New York: Simon & Schuster, 1978.

Committee on the Evolution of Work. *The Changing Situation of Workers and Their Unions.* Washington, D.C.: AFL-CIO, 1985.

Committee on the Evolution of Work. *The Future of Work.* Washington, D.C.: AFL-CIO, 1983.

Craypo, Charles. *The Economics of Collective Bargaining: Case Studies in the Private Sector.* Washington, D.C.: The Bureau of National Affairs, Inc., 1986.

Dunlop, John T., and Chamberlain, Neil W. *Frontiers of Collective Bargaining.* New York: Harper & Row, 1967.

Economics Education Project. *Crises in the Public Sector.* New York: Monthly Review Press, 1983.

Edwards, Richard C.; Reich, Michael; and Weisskopf, Thomas E. *The Capitalist System.* Englewood Cliffs, N.J.: Prentice-Hall, 1973.

Elkouri, Edna A., and Elkouri, Frank. *How Arbitration Works.* 4th ed. Washington, D.C.: Bureau of National Affairs, 1985.

Estey, Martin. The Unions: Structure, Development, and Management. 3rd ed. New York: Harcourt Brace Jovanovich, 1981.

Fillipelli, Ronald. *Labor in the U.S.A.: A History.* New York: Alfred A. Knopf, 1984.

Foner, Philip S. *History of the Labor Movement in the United States,* Vols. 1 and 2. New York: International Publishers, 1947, 1955.

Freeman, Richard B., and Medoff, James L. *What Do Unions Do.* New York: Basic Books, 1984.

Fuentes, Annette and Ehrenreich, Barbara. *Women in the Global Factory.* Boston: South End Press, 1983.

Galenson, Walter. *The CIO Challenge to the AFL: A History of the American Labor Movement, 1935–1941.* Cambridge, Mass.: Harvard University Press, 1960.

Getman, Julius G. *Labor Relations: Law, Practice, and Policy.* Mineola, N.Y.: Foundation Press, 1978.

Gifford, Courtney D. *Directory of U.S. Labor Organizations, 1984–85 Edition.* Washington, D.C.: Bureau of National Affairs, 1984.

Gorman, Robert A. *Basic Text on Labor Law: Unionization and Collective Bargaining.* St. Paul, Minn.: West Publishing Co., 1976.

Harrington, Michael. *The New American Poverty.* New York: Penguin Books, 1984.

Hershfield, David. *The Multinational Union Challenges the Multinational Company.* New York: Conference Board, Inc., 1975.

Jones, James M. *Prejudice and Racism.* Reading, Mass.: Addison-Wesley Publishing Co., 1972.

Josephson, Matthew. *The Robber Barons: The Great American Capitalists, 1861–1901.* New York: Harcourt, Brace, & World, Inc., 1934.

Juris, Hervey; Thompson, Mark; and Daniels, Wilbur, eds. *Industrial Relations in a Decade of Economic Change.* Madison: Industrial Relations Research Association, 1985.

Justice, Betty. *Unions, Workers, and the Law.* Washington, D.C.: The Bureau of National Affairs, Inc., 1983.

Kassalow, Everett M. *Trade Unions and Industrial Relations: An International Comparison.* New York: Random House, 1969.

Kerr, Clark; Dunlop, John T.; Harbison, Frederick; and Myers, Charles A. *Industrialism and Industrial Man.* Cambridge, Mass.: Harvard University Press, 1960.

Kochan, Thomas A. *Challenges and Choices Facing American Labor.* Cambridge: The MIT Press, 1985.

Laslett, John. *Labor and the Left: A Study of Socialist and Radical Influences in the American Labor Movement, 1881–1924.* New York: Basic Books, 1970.

Lekackman, Robert, and Von Loon, Borin. *Capitalism for Beginners.* New York: Pantheon Books, 1981.

Lester, Richard A. *Economics of Labor.* New York: Macmillan Co., 1964.

Levine, Marvin J., and Hagburg, Eugene C. *Public Sector Labor Relations.* St. Paul, Minn.: West Publishing Co., 1979.

Lynd, Staughton. *Labor Law for the Rank and Filer.* Singlejack Little Book Series. San Pedro, Cal.: Miles & Weir, 1978.

Marshall, F. Ray. *The Negro and Organized Labor.* New York: John Wiley & Sons, 1965.

Marshall, F. Ray; Briggs, Vernon M.; and King, Allan G. *Labor Economics.* 5th ed. Homewood, Ill.: Irwin Press, 1984.

Marshall, F. Ray, and Perlman, Richard. An Anthology of Labor Economics: Readings and Commentary. New York: John Wiley & Sons, 1972.

Morris, Charles J., ed. *The Developing Labor Law: The Board, the Courts, and the National Labor Relations Act.* 2nd ed., with supplements. Washington, D.C.: The Bureau of National Affairs, Inc., 1983.

Morris, Richard B. *The American Worker.* Washington, D.C.: Government Printing Office, 1977.

Naffziger, Fred J., and Knauss, Keith. *A Basic Guide to Federal Labor Law.* Columbus, Ohio: Grid Publishing, 1975.

Needleman, Ruth, ed., Turning the Tide: Women, Unions, and Labor Education, theme issue. *Labor Studies Journal,* Winter, 1986.

Montgomery, David. *Workers Control in America.* Cambridge: Cambridge University Press, 1979.

Pierson, Frank C. *Unions in Postwar America.* New York: Random House, 1967.

Rayback, Joseph G. *A History of American Labor.* New York: Free Press, 1966.

Repas, Bob. *Contract Administration: A Guide for Stewards and Local Officers.* Washington, D.C.: The Bureau of National Affairs, Inc., 1984.

Richardson, Reed C. *Collective Bargaining by Objectives.* Englewood Cliffs, N.J.: Prentice-Hall, 1977.

Rius. *Marx for Beginners.* New York: Pantheon Books, 1976.

Schlossberg, Stephen I., and Sherman, Frederick E. *Organizing and the Law.* Washington, D.C.: The Bureau of National Affairs, Inc., 1971.

Schnapper, M. B. *American Labor, A Pictorial Social History.* Washington, D.C.: Public Affairs Press, 1972.

Shister, Joseph. *Economics of the Labor Market.* Philadelphia: J. B. Lippincott Co., 1956.

Slaughter, Jane. *Concessions and How to Beat Them.* Detroit: Labor Education and Research Project, 1983.

Sloane, Arthur, and Witney, Fred. *Labor Relations.* 5th ed. Englewood Cliffs, N.J.: Prentice-Hall, 1985.

Smith, Russell A.; Merrifield, Leroy S.; and St. Antoine, Theodor J. *Labor Relations Law.* 4th ed., with supplement. Indianapolis: Bobbs-Merrill Co., 1968.

Sturmthal, Adolf. *Comparative Labor Movements.* Belmont, Cal.: Wadsworth Publishing Co., 1972.

Summers, Clyde W., and Wellington, Harry H. *Labor Law: Cases and Materials.* Mineola, N.Y.: Foundation Press, 1968.

Taft, Philip. *The AF of L in the Time of Gompers.* New York: Harper & Brothers, 1957.

________. *Organized Labor in American History.* New York: Harper & Row, 1964.

Taylor, Benjamin J., and Witney, Fred. *Labor Relations Law.* Englewood Cliffs, N.J.: Prentice-Hall, 1971.

Tierney, James, and Tucker, Ralph. *Workers Guide to Labor Law.* Orono, Me.: Bureau of Labor Education, 1974.

Uhlman, Lloyd. *American Trade Unionism—Past and Present.* Berkeley, Cal.: Institute of Industrial Relations, University of California, 1961.

U.S. Department of Labor, Bureau of Labor Statistics, *Brief History of the American Labor Movement.* Rev. ed. Washington, D.C.: Government Printing Office, 1976.

________. *Directory of National Unions and Employee Associations, 1977.* Bulletin No. 2044. Washington, D.C.: Government Printing Office, 1979.

Wallihan, James. *Union Government and Organization.* Washington, D.C.: The Bureau of National Affairs, Inc., 1985.

Weber, Arnold R., ed. *The Structure of Collective Bargaining.* New York: Free Press of Glencoe, 1961.

Wertheimer, Barbara Mayer. *We Were There: The Story of Working Women in America.* New York: Pantheon Books, Div. of Random House, 1977.

Whittaker, William G. *The Common Situs Picketing Issue: Background and Activity in the 94th Congress.* Washington, D.C.: Library of Congress, Congressional Research Service, 1976.

Wortman, Max S., Jr. *Critical Issues in Labor.* New York: Macmillan Co., 1969.

Zinn, Howard. *A People's History of the United States.* New York: Harper & Row, 1980.

Topical Index

D

E

F

M

N

O

P

About the Author

Lee Balliet has been Director of the Division of Labor Studies at Indiana University since 1982. Prior to his current position, he worked for labor education programs at West Virginia University, the University of Kentucky, and the University of Wisconsin. He earned his doctorate in economics, under F. Ray Marshall, at the University of Texas and worked for several years as a private consultant to unions and government agencies. Dr. Balliet has been a union member and activist in workers education for over 30 years.